FROM ALAN MAKEY
KENT FHS HON.EDITOR
29 THE MALL, FAVERSHAM
KENT ME13 8JL

# Roots in Three Counties

A history of the Hansford family

of Dorset, Kent & Lancashire.

Compiled and Researched

By

Beverley Hansford

Matador
9 Priory Business Park,
Wistow Road, Kibworth Beauchamp,
Leicestershire. LE8 0RX
Tel: (+44) 116 279 2299
Fax: (+44) 116 279 2277
Email: books@troubador.co.uk
Web: www.troubador.co.uk/matador


ISBN 9781 780882 512

British Library Cataloguing in Publication Data.
A catalogue record for this book is available from the British Library.

Typeset in 12pt Perpetua by Troubador Publishing Ltd, Leicester, UK

**Matador** is an imprint of Troubador Publishing Ltd


Printed in Great Britain by the MPG Books Group, Bodmin and King's Lynn

*This book is dedicated to all my ancestors*
*for living their lives*
*with such inspiration and bravery.*

# CONTENTS

**PART 3**                                                               **131**

# PREFACE

In all research, a point is reached at which a calculated decision has to be made: whether the findings are ready to be shared with a wider audience. Usually this decision will be taken when the researcher has produced results that present fresh, reliable and valid information.

Family history is no stranger to this decision-making. The dedicated family historian will have to decide when the time is right for the information so diligently gleaned to be presented to other interested parties. Usually this will be when the researcher has amassed a considerable amount of knowledge about his or her family history and possesses an accurate picture of the lives of the key members of the family over the centuries. Inevitably by this stage the research will have slowed down and 'finds' be less frequent. There will also be the feeling that certain areas of research may require a considerable amount of time and effort, and that the answers to some questions may never be found, because the information is just not available.

This was the situation I found myself in a short time ago. I had spent ten years researching my family and now had a fairly clear picture of who they were, where they came from and what they did. For the most part, my research was fully confirmed by official documentation. True, there were gaps in the story – including ancestors who seemed to completely vanish from the records – but in comparison to the whole these were of a minor nature.

It became abundantly clear that the time was now ripe to put pen to paper and write everything up. To delay would achieve very little, and any further information that came to light could quite easily be incorporated into future editions. Therefore, the research is not considered to be finished, which means that this document is presented as part work already completed and part 'work in progress'. Indeed, it is possible that the very act of publishing this family history will lead to some of the mysteries being solved.

# PART 1

*The Original Family Tree*

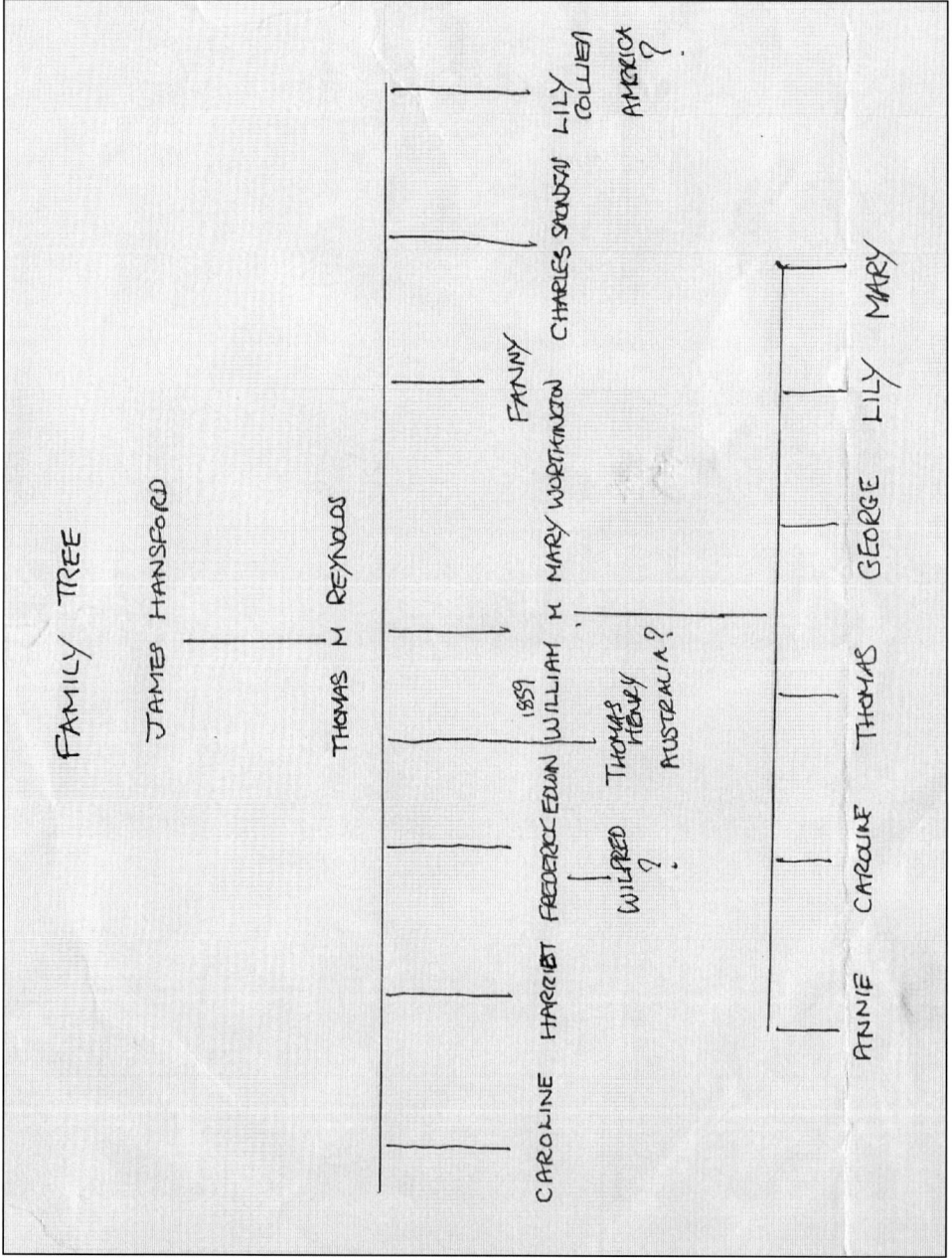

FAMILY TREE

JAMES HANSFORD

THOMAS M REYNOLDS

CAROLINE HARRIET FREDERICK EDWIN WILLIAM M MARY WORTHINGTON FANNY CHARLES SAUNDERS LILY (COLLIER)

1859

WILFRED ? THOMAS HENRY AUSTRALIA ? AMERICA ?

ANNIE CAROLINE THOMAS GEORGE LILY MARY

# HOW IT ALL BEGAN

Before I started researching my family history, I knew very little about my ancestors. Unusually, my parents rarely spoke about their families, except for the odd comment here and there.

I knew that my mother had been born in the village of Oulton in the West Riding of Yorkshire and that my father had been born and brought up in the Lancashire town of Wigan, but that was about as much information as I had about their early life. I was also aware that I had aunts, uncles and cousins in both counties, but any contact with them had been extremely limited. Until adult life, I had not given a great deal of thought to the fact that I had never met any of my grandparents. Perhaps my parents opting to live many miles from their roots contributed to this situation.

It was against this background that I had my first contact with family history. The time was the mid-sixties, and I was living in St Albans. My parents were retired and living in Leeds, and on one of my monthly visits to them I received the information that proved to be the starting point for my interest in family history research.

It was a glorious summer weekend, and over a quiet drink one evening with my parents somehow the question of family roots came up. Up until that point I had always imagined my father coming from a long line of Hansfords, all resident in Wigan and toiling away in that industrial town. My father quickly dispelled that theory. I listened, enthralled, as he told me that the family were relative newcomers to the area. They were, he said, 'seafaring folk', who had come to Wigan from Chatham, Kent. The reason for their move was even more intriguing. It had been prompted by 'some sort of catastrophe' in the family. My father related more details. It appeared that several brothers had been lost at sea on the same ship, and the surviving brother, his great-grandfather James Hansford, had decided that the family would move away from the sea and sever all connections with it, in order that 'none of the children would have the urge or opportunity to go to sea'. Indeed, my father revealed that it was the practice in the family that the children were never taken to the seaside.

I was fascinated by the story. It was all new and exciting. So many questions raced through my mind. Why were the brothers all on one ship? How had they been lost? My father could give me no more information. That was as much as he knew. But that fact did not dampen my enthusiasm to know more. I resolved that one day I would find the answers to my questions.

I was so intrigued with what I had heard, that, with my father looking over my shoulder, I drew up a rough family tree on a piece of paper, based on what he could tell me. Somehow I knew that when the time came to undertake the task of delving deeper into the story, that tiny piece of paper would be a key factor. It would be an invaluable starting point.

Little did I know then that many years would pass before I would be able to fulfil my dream and utilise the information I had written down that day.

# STARTING OUT

I looked after the scrap of paper with the details of my ancestors on it very carefully. Occasionally I would come across it and think again about my plans to find out more one day, but always it seemed the time was not right. Work and day-to-day living demanded precedence.

Many years passed and it was not until my semi-retirement in the year 2000 that I turned my thoughts once again to family history. I took out that piece of paper and looked at it. It had become torn and yellowed with age, but the information on it remained good. I decided that the time had arrived when I must carry out the plans I had made over forty years previously. I knew that if I did not start then, the task would never be completed.

By this time family history had become one of the UK's most popular hobbies. Everybody, it seemed, wanted to know more about their roots. There was plenty of material to assist researchers: books and magazines were in abundance and there were family history societies in most counties, with a wealth of experience and help to draw upon.

So it was that I set out. I decided to research the male line of my family, which of course carries the name Hansford forward in each generation.

I knew that it is the usual practice to start with oneself and work backwards. One's parents' marriage certificate should indicate the names of one's two grandfathers, and from there it is possible to track backwards, collecting birth, marriage and death certificates on the way. That is fine for all events after the beginning of 1837, the year civil registration commenced in England and Wales and the official recording of births, deaths and marriages became obligatory. For events prior to that date, it is a case of looking at the parish or church records, and this is when the task becomes slightly more complicated and the information less reliable. Nevertheless, it is possible to build up a picture of a family's history back through quite a number of years. The various censuses available to researchers, starting with the year 1841 and carried out every ten years since (excluding 1941), are an excellent check on where people were on a particular date, where they were born and what they did for a living; and, because they also list any children in the household, they can be a very useful resource for filling in detail.

Armed with all this information, I was ready to begin. I was aware of the Guild of One-Name Studies and I thought it might be a good idea to write to this organisation and ask if any research had taken place on my surname. I received a reply giving the name and address of my local contact, who lived in Middlesex. I immediately wrote a second letter outlining my research plans. Several days later, I received a telephone call from Michael Hansford, who introduced himself as the contact person in my area. He asked me what I had done in the way of research so far, and when I admitted that my entire knowledge to date consisted of a few names on a bit of paper, he helpfully suggested that I send him a list of these and he would check his own records and see if he could help.

A few days later, a letter arrived from Michael. Not only had he checked out the names, but he had also listed the reference numbers to enable me to order a copy of these ancestors' birth certificates. With this information, I would be able to build up a fairly good picture of not only my father's brother and sisters, but also his parents. It would be a really good start to my research.

It was a rather grey and miserable November afternoon when I made my way to the Family Records Centre (FRC) in Myddelton Street, Islington, London. As this was in the time before records became widely available on the internet, when I arrived there the centre was crowded. I made my way in the direction indicated by an official at the reception desk and found myself in a large search room made up almost entirely of shelves containing large ledger-type books. In between the rows of shelves were tables to place the books on for reading.

I soon got the hang of things. The books were in three colours: red for births, green for marriages and black for deaths. First I needed to locate the year I wanted to look at. As registrations are listed in quarters, there were four books to a year. Next I had to locate the correct letter of the alphabet. I trawled down the alphabetical list of surnames in each volume, and when I discovered what appeared to be the right person I made a note of the reference number and the registration district, plus the year and the quarter. And that was all there was to it. I carefully checked the reference numbers on the list Michael had given me. As I expected, they were all correct. It was then necessary to complete a form for each certificate I required. I wanted a lot: copies of the birth certificates for aunts and an uncle I had never met. It took me a little time to fill in all the required forms and then print my name and address on one of the envelopes provided. I queued up to place my order and when it was my turn the woman behind the desk checked my forms and ran them through a machine. She told me the certificates would be posted to me within a week. I paid the fee with my credit card and decided to celebrate by having a coffee in the restaurant downstairs. My family history research was under way.

That was the first of numerous visits I made to Myddelton Street. I was to spend many hours looking at those books. Sometimes my patience was rewarded; at other times I had little in the way of results to show for my efforts. Sadly, the FRC closed its doors to the public in 2008 as a result of cuts in government spending. Certain records were moved to the publicly accessible National Archives at Kew, but those splendid and useful books were moved to a closed archive, and the atmosphere of the FRC was gone forever.

Six days after my first visit, an envelope arrived containing copies of all the certificates I had ordered. My tatty bit of paper was now slowly transforming into a proper family tree. It was almost as if flesh were being put on the bones of a skeleton. I now had a much better picture of my father's immediate family. It was time to move on to the previous generation.

# EARLY RESEARCH: PROBLEMS AND SURPRISES

Over the next few months I progressed steadily, piecing together a picture of my father's family in Wigan. I made regular visits to the Family Records Centre, carried out research and ordered more certificates. Things were going well and though there were still many gaps to fill regarding my ancestors' time in Wigan, I considered it was now time to investigate the next generation on my scrap of paper, represented by my great-grandfather Thomas Henry Hansford.

I had obtained an extract from the 1881 census, a transcript of the original documents carried out by The Church of Jesus Christ of Latter-day Saints, more commonly known as Mormons. Members of the church are encouraged to research their family history, and the church has built up a substantial database of births, marriages and deaths at its headquarters in Salt Lake City, USA. Family History Centres have been set up within many of their temples in the UK, and these are open to the public. Due to its unique method of transcription the 1881 census is a valuable tool for the family historian because it is possible to immediately identify a surname in a particular area without laborious searching of page after page of census returns.

The transcript showed Thomas Henry Hansford living with his family at 4 Miry Lane, Wigan. From this record I was able to work out the approximate date of his marriage. From the details given to me by my father, I knew that Thomas Henry had married a woman with the surname Reynolds. The 1881 census shows her first names as Harriet E. Very often the birth of the first child gives a clue to the date of a Victorian marriage. This was the hunch that I followed and in this case it paid off. More searching among those books at the FRC revealed that Thomas Henry had married in 1850. Immediately I ordered a copy of the marriage certificate.

It was when this document arrived that I encountered the first of the puzzles that are such a familiar part of family history research. The copy certificate showed that Thomas Henry Hansford had married Harriet Eliza Reynolds on 17 November 1850 in St John the

Evangelist church, Waterloo, London. However, the details conflicted with the information I already had. Waterloo is some distance from Wigan and indeed Chatham. My father had clearly stated that it was James Hansford, Thomas Henry's father, who had migrated north from Chatham. So if Thomas Henry was supposed to be in Wigan, what was he doing in London? There were two even more puzzling pieces of information on the certificate. Thomas Henry's father's name was recorded as John, not James, and his occupation as 'iron moulder'. According to my father he was a sailor. On top of this, the 1881 census gave Thomas Henry's birthplace as Clapthon – a place I had never heard of.

I wasted some time on this alleged place of birth. It seemed logical – or so I thought – that it might just be a misspelling of Clapham. I made my first visit to the London Metropolitan Archives (LMA), which holds the parish records for London. The relative quiet of this establishment was a pleasant change from the activity of the FRC. At that time it did not receive the volume of visitors it does today.

Most of the records I wanted to look at were on microfilm. It was necessary to obtain each film from a cabinet and then load it into a film reader, which projected its contents onto a screen. Advancing and rewinding the film was by a hand-operated winder. Going through a complete film in this way is a slow process and, to add to the frustration, occasionally the quality is not very good and parts are almost impossible to read. Fortunately I only wanted to look at records around the year 1830, so that cut down the time considerably.

However, my research at the LMA revealed nought. Thomas Henry was certainly not born in Clapham. It was at that point that I remembered the golden rule of family history research: if there is a query like this, always go back to the original source to check. I needed to look at the original census. The document I had been looking at was a transcript. It meant another visit to the FRC. I knew that copies of the entire census from 1841 to 1881 were available there. When I arrived, I made my way to the first floor and found a film reader. I obtained the correct film for the 1881 census for Wigan, and ten minutes' viewing provided my answer. Thomas Henry's place of birth was quite clearly written – Chatham. I had been caught out by a simple transcription error. But what was important to me was the location. So the trail was leading back to Chatham. I could not wait to check Thomas Henry's birth details. As the date in question was around 1830, I would have to go back to the Kent parish records. These were held in Strood, which is not far from Chatham.

I set off early one wet morning in late spring. It was about a two-and-a-half-hour train journey to Strood, with a change of stations in London. It was close to 9 o'clock when I arrived at Strood. It was still raining quite heavily, and to make matters worse a gusty wind had got up. I walked in what I thought would be the direction of the record office and after going wrong briefly once, I found it without too much difficulty. It was tucked away behind the town hall, close to the river Medway, on which the closely linked towns of Rochester and Chatham are also situated.

I was the first researcher to arrive, and a friendly middle-aged woman ushered me to a film reader and explained the layout and facilities of the record office. It did not take me long to locate the correct film from the filing cabinet where they were all stored, and then it was down to work. Twenty minutes later I had my answers. On 28 March 1830, Thomas Henry, son of James and Eliza Hansford, was baptised in St Mary's parish church, Chatham. One of the most revealing features of the entry was that Thomas Henry's father's occupation was given as 'seaman'. So my father had been correct: the family had lived in Chatham and there had been connections with the sea.

I left the Strood record office feeling highly pleased with the day's research. Not only had I cleared up several queries, but in addition I had learned another very important aspect of family history research: even official documents such as marriage certificates can contain incorrect information. Our Victorian ancestors were sometimes not completely honest about the information they gave, quite often because they simply did not know the correct answer. In Thomas Henry's case, as will be revealed later, it is highly likely that he did not know his father's occupation, so he made a calculated guess. His father died when Thomas Henry was only three, and his mother died when he was eight. An orphan brought up by other members of the family and sometimes by strangers, he may have felt that his ancestry was of little importance.

Over the next few months I spent time collecting more information, sending for birth and marriage certificates for Thomas Henry's family; all were readily obtainable, as they were post-1837. The task entailed spending time at the FRC going through the record books again, but that was part of the pleasure.

It was when I came to research James, Thomas Henry's father, that more complex questions needed to be unravelled. At first it was extremely difficult to find out any more about him. It was hard to know where to start looking. Seeing him described first as an iron moulder and then as a seaman made me wonder whether he had been employed at Chatham dockyard. It seemed a reasonable line of thought to follow up. However, the records of the naval dockyards were kept in the National Archives at Kew, which meant making my first visit to this establishment.

On a fine spring morning I made my way to the archives, which are housed in a purpose-built facility close to the river Thames. In those days the National Archives had a more reserved atmosphere than today. Newcomers had to learn the complicated procedure attached to looking at original documents. First, a reader's card had to be obtained, and this had to be applied for via a computer terminal in the foyer. This was a rather daunting task for those who, like me at that stage, were not well versed in the use of computers. It took me several attempts to complete the task and I narrowly missed having the allocated time run out. However, once I had succeeded, it was a simple process to collect my reader's card from the enquiry desk.

Following that first encounter with a computer, it came as no surprise to me to find out that all documents had to be ordered via a computer terminal, after obtaining the reference details. On my first attempt I did not realise that I needed to select a seat number beforehand. If this is not done, the order is rejected. Once I had overcome this minor obstacle, all went well. Twenty minutes later I picked up a large cardboard box from the collection desk.

When I opened the box, it revealed a large ledger-type book, carefully scripted by a Victorian clerk almost two hundred years previously. When one has the privilege of looking at original documents like these, one might be tempted to wonder about the lives of the people who so carefully wrote down the details, and how they would view our way of life.

I went carefully through that book, then another and another. One thing became clear: James had not worked at Chatham dockyard.

I mused over the situation. I knew there was an answer somewhere, but where? The breakthrough came one evening when I had been discussing the situation with Michael. About half an hour after we finished talking, he called me back. 'I think I may have found something,' he said. 'I've found a James Hansford who was in the navy.' It sounded too good to be true, and it completely changed the view of things. I had taken 'seafaring' to denote the merchant fleet. The navy had not occurred to me up until this point.

This new information meant a return visit to Kew. This time I was able to quickly find what I was looking for. A James Hansford had served in the navy for a period of ten years, ending abruptly in August 1833. There did not seem to be any further information available. What was the next step?

Something – perhaps it was intuition – made me return to the record office at Strood. I felt I needed to look again at the microfilmed records of St Mary's church, Chatham. After about an hour I found what I was looking for: a burial record for James Hansford, aged 30. The date was 24 August 1833, only a few days after his discharge from his last ship. I was intrigued by a small note alongside his burial entry. I noticed similar notes on other pages. I had difficulty in deciphering it. I asked for help from one of the staff, who in turn called the head archivist. The head archivist looked at the notation for a few seconds and then said simply 'Cholera'. So that was the answer. That was why James's naval career had ended suddenly. But the find indicated one important fact. My father had been incorrect in saying that it was James who had taken the family north to Wigan. It was impossible: James died long before the move was made. This raised a question. Who had brought Thomas Henry up?

I put research into Thomas Henry's early life on hold while I busied myself finding out more about my immediate ancestors. Eventually I was prodded into taking it up again by a chance remark by one of my cousins. One of the bonuses of researching the family history was that I had been reunited with my four cousins, three of whom still lived in Wigan. It was during a telephone conversation that one of them gave me a clue for the next stage. While we were talking about my research and discussing our ancestors, my cousin remarked casually, 'I think one of them went to Greenwich School.' This set me thinking. The Royal Hospital School at Greenwich was run for the sons and daughters of naval seamen; very often these children were orphans. Thomas Henry had been orphaned at an early age. It was a possibility definitely worth following up, and that meant another trip to Kew, where the naval records were kept.

On a bright summer morning I made my way yet again to the National Archives. By now, with a few visits behind me, I had 'acquired the knowledge', and ordering documents presented no problems. I quickly looked up the reference number of the document I wanted to view. It did not take long to find: ADM73/247, Admissions to Greenwich Royal Hospital School, surnames Hams-Hare. I ordered the document and went and had a cup of coffee while I waited for it to arrive at the collection desk.

When I collected my order it turned out to be a large rectangular cardboard box securely tied with tapes. Inside was a separate folder for each applicant, containing the relevant papers. On the outside of each folder the name of the applicant was clearly written. I started to make my way through the contents of the box. There were a lot of folders. After about an hour, I had perused about half of the box's contents. I was beginning to wonder whether this line of enquiry would turn out to be another damp squib and whether I would return home once again with no answers to Thomas Henry's background. Then I saw the name on the next folder: HANSFORD. I quickly placed it on one side, only to see a second folder with the name on it, followed by a third and a fourth. In all I retrieved about half a dozen folders with the family name on them from the box. With almost shaking hands I started to read their contents. It did not take me long to realise that at least four of the folders related to my family. But the greatest excitement came from the fact that I had experienced one of those rare moments in family history research when there is a momentous discovery. In my hands I held details not only of Thomas Henry, but also of his father and his grandfather. The folders contained invaluable details of the naval careers of these men as well as information about their families.

When I left Kew that day, I felt as if I were walking on air. My family history research had been given new impetus: my find had moved me beyond the first name on my original bit of paper and had added a new generation. I now felt that I had the beginnings of a family tree. True, there were many gaps, and hundreds of questions needed answers, but I was going in the right direction.

Such an exciting day was never to be repeated. After that it was down to the hard work of many hours of research, sometimes with the satisfaction of coming across new material, but frequently with no finds to record. I visited other record offices, following up clues or researching individual ancestors. The gaps in the family tree were slowly beginning to be filled in. I contacted other researchers, sometimes receiving new information, sometimes providing them with data from my records.

In those early years I discovered a lot about researching family history. I learned the golden rule: never accept anything as accurate without checking the original source of the information. I learned never to throw anything away. Time and again, I found some snippet of information and filed it, thinking it was not important or did not relate to my family, only to find out later that it proved to be a valuable piece of the research.

Family history is rather like completing a jigsaw puzzle: you pick up a piece and it will not fit, put it on one side and then later find it is the very piece you are looking for in a new part of the picture.

# THE RESEARCH BECOMES MORE INTENSE

Over the next few years I plodded steadily on with my research. I was beginning to feel quite pleased with my results: no longer was my family history a blank page, I could trace my ancestors back to the 1770s and I now had a fairly good picture in my mind of how they lived their lives. The family tree had grown considerably since that scrap of paper I had started out with.

Every week I would spend a day in London, peering at films on a screen at the Family Records Centre or the London Metropolitan Archives or deciphering copperplate handwriting in dusty record books at Kew. It became quite a compulsion. Sometimes I was lucky and found a snippet of information to add to my collection; at other times, after spending hours searching, I came away empty-handed. But I had long since realised that family history research is not all plain sailing. Like many other family historians I spoke to, I discovered little areas of research that were extremely difficult to unravel, despite repeated attempts to find answers. Some of these investigations dragged on for years before the mystery was suddenly solved; others have questions surrounding them to this day.

The following family members fall into the above category and perhaps illustrate the dedication and patience required by the family historian.

## HARRIET ELIZA REYNOLDS

In spite of the steady progress I had made, there were several ancestors who seemed unwilling to reveal themselves. One of these was my great-grandmother Harriet Eliza, who was married to Thomas Henry Hansford. Though I was researching the male line of my family, I did not want to ignore their wives completely; it is always nice – and often helpful – to have a little background information on the spouses. I had been quite successful in this respect, even as far back as my great-great-great-grandmother Elizabeth Colliver, who married James

Hansford in 1796. However, my great-grandmother remained aloof; it appeared that she did not want to be discovered. This was odd, because at the start I had thought she would be one of the easiest wives to trace. Even my father had known that she was born Harriet Eliza Reynolds, and as his grandmother she would almost certainly have been around when he was a small boy.

My starting point was the 1881 census, in which Harriet Eliza had stated that she was born in Greenwich. It seemed quite logical; my family had associations with that area of Kent as well as Chatham. As Harriet Eliza was born around 1832, before official records started, any information about her birth would have to be obtained from church records. I made another visit to the London Metropolitan Archives (LMA), where all the records for London churches are kept. The main church in Greenwich is St Alfege, a delightful old building in the centre of the town, now sadly hemmed in by traffic. Several of Thomas Henry and Harriet Eliza's children were baptised there during the 1850s.

In the low lighting of the LMA I spent many hours and several visits peering into a film reader and searching for Harriet Eliza's birth details. The records of St Alfege revealed nothing. Not content with that, I started searching the records of adjoining parishes. In the end I covered all the parishes from Greenwich to Lambeth without success. So where was Harriet Eliza born? It was a mystery.

Very often in family history research, when one comes up against a blank wall like this, it is useful to have a second look at the documents already collected. One day, with this strategy in mind, I scrutinised Thomas Henry and Harriet Eliza's wedding certificate. I was intrigued by the names of the two witnesses: Thomas and Elizabeth Reynolds. A coincidence? Unlikely. The find made me search deeper into the records for the church of St John the Evangelist, Waterloo, where the marriage had taken place. I did not have to look far. Seven years previously, on 21 May 1843, Thomas Reynolds, widower, and Elizabeth Squires, widow, had also married there. Harriet Eliza at that time would have been 10 or 11 years old, so it seemed that Thomas Reynolds might not have been her father. There might well have been a previous marriage, and to establish this, further investigation into Elizabeth Squires' background would be necessary.

Finding Elizabeth in the records proved to be quite easy. On the 1851 census her place of birth is recorded as 'Surrey Kingston'. This could only have been Kingston upon Thames. In the early days of my family history research efforts, I had joined the Society of Genealogists and this proved to be a useful asset on this occasion. Half an hour in their library searching through the transcripts of Kingston births gave me the information I required. Elizabeth Squires, daughter of Timothy and Mary Squires, was born on 14 February 1804.

This gave more credence to something I had spotted previously. On the 1841 census for Greenwich I had come across a Thomas Reynolds living with an Elizabeth Squires. There were also three children listed: Mary, aged 15, Caroline, aged 10, and Harriet, aged 5. Elizabeth's age was about right for a birth in 1804, and if the '5' in the column for Harriet's age was in fact a badly formed '8', the youngest of the three children could be 'my' Harriet Eliza. It looked as if I had discovered Thomas Reynolds and Elizabeth Squires two years before their marriage. I could not make out Thomas's occupation, but Elizabeth described herself as a charwoman. Perhaps Thomas was making a home for Elizabeth and her children and at the same time providing himself with a housekeeper. It seemed a logical explanation.

This bit of research threw up another question. When did Thomas Henry Hansford meet the Reynolds family? He was at Greenwich Royal Hospital School from September 1841 to May 1845. From the census I knew that Thomas Reynolds and Elizabeth Squires were in Greenwich in 1841, but their marriage certificate indicates that they were living in Lambeth in 1843. This suggests that Thomas Henry got to know the Reynolds family early on in his time at the school. Perhaps they met and took pity on the orphaned boy from Chatham, isolated from his brother and sister and having to cope with the strange environment of a naval school. Certainly Thomas Henry appears to have been taken under the wing of the family. It may have been that his future father-in-law arranged vocational training for him when he left school, and that he then lived with and became part of the family, growing up alongside his future wife Harriet Eliza.

One aspect of the Harriet Eliza story has always intrigued me. It produced a question that I had hoped and almost expected would be answered by the research. This was the appearance of the name Saunders in the family tree. Thomas Henry and Harriet Eliza named one of their sons Charles Saunders. It was not unusual for our Victorian ancestors to do this, as they liked their children to carry on the surname of their grandparents. This was the case with one of their daughters, whom they christened Elizabeth Reynolds. No need to ask where that second name came from. I fully expected to turn up ancestors somewhere with the surname Saunders. Nothing seemed to fit in on the male side, so I reckoned it must have come from Harriet Eliza's family. Had her mother previously been married to a man named Saunders, the details lost in old documents somewhere? As yet I have found no record of any such marriage. Had there been a common-law arrangement? This happened even in Victorian times. Perhaps at some point in the future the answer will leap out of some dusty book or when I am looking for something else on the computer. For the present it remains one of those unsolved and intriguing mysteries.

**THOMAS REYNOLDS**

I could not leave the whole episode without taking a look at Thomas Reynolds' background. It was a surprise to find him listed on the 1851 census as a 'Greenwich Pensioner'. This indicated that he had had a naval career. To find out more another search in the National Archives at Kew was necessary. I found what I thought was my man, only to discover after several visits that things did not quite seem to work out. In my enthusiasm I had followed up the wrong naval record. Apparently there were two men named Thomas Reynolds with naval careers at about the same time. I retraced my steps and eventually found the one I wanted. 'My' Thomas served twelve years in the Royal Navy, retiring on a pension in 1842, the year before he married Elizabeth Squires. I managed to check that I had the right man by doing a cross-reference on his place of birth. On the 1851 census this appears as Walsall, Staffordshire. The naval records give the same location. Naval records were of course never intended to be used for family history research, but their detail makes them extremely useful for anyone looking for information about ancestors who were in the navy.

With the aid of records held by the Society of Genealogists I managed to find a little bit more about Thomas's background. The son of John and Isabella Reynolds, he was baptised at St Matthew's church, Walsall, Staffordshire on 27 December 1786. His naval record confirms that Elizabeth Squires was not his first wife, but to date I have been unable to obtain details of any previous marriage. According to the naval records it looks as if he died in 1863, as that is the year his pension ceased. Elizabeth died in 1864 from a 'tumour in the neck and apoplexy'.

**ELEANOR ELIZABETH HANSFORD**

I first encountered Eleanor early on in my research during one of my visits to the record office at Strood. I came across her name unexpectedly when I was looking for something else. The details on the film I was reading were quite simple: admission to Medway Union Workhouse on 22 May 1889 – Eleanor Hansford and her five children with ages ranging from 2 to 11 years.

The entry interested me because of the surname, but at that time I did not relate Eleanor to my family and it was just an item of interest that I copied down and put away for safe keeping: one of those bits of the jigsaw puzzle that did not fit into the picture at the time.

Eventually, after a good deal more research and several false leads, I managed to trace the story of Eleanor and her family. I relate it here in some detail because I think it illustrates fully the kind of life our Victorian ancestors sometimes had to endure, and the fragility of their existence.

Eleanor (her second name Elizabeth only occurs on her birth documents) was a granddaughter of Amelia, one of James Hansford senior's daughters. She was born on 31 July 1853, apparently out of wedlock. Illegitimacy appears to have run in the family, as there is no record of a marriage for her mother or her grandmother.

What is interesting in the case of Eleanor is that her father's name appears on her birth certificate: William Burton, a lieutenant in the Royal Marines. We cannot be sure whether he consented to being registered as her father, or whether her mother, when asked the question, innocently gave his name. Perhaps she expected him to marry her eventually; certainly she seemed to know quite a lot about him, and this would tend to indicate that the relationship was more than a one-night event.

Eleanor was born at a time when the family fortunes, if not high, were stable and sustaining. Her mother and grandmother, both named Amelia, appeared to live together throughout her mother's life. Their income was supplemented for a while by contributions from Eleanor's great-grandfather James, who spent the last years of his life with the family after Eleanor's great-grandmother died in 1840. Samuel, Amelia's younger brother, lived with her in the 1860s until his death in 1869, and probably contributed to the family's finances.

What about the main family income? This is where the story becomes intriguing. On all the census returns from 1851 to 1871, Eleanor's mother, grandmother and sister (yet another Amelia) all gave their occupation as 'dressmaker'. Now they may well have been dressmakers, but, as another family history researcher pointed out to me, it was a useful ploy for a prostitute of the day to list herself as a dressmaker when the census enumerator came knocking on the door. Personally I believe the three Amelias were indeed dressmakers, though it could well be that they supplemented their income by selling their favours when times were hard or opportunity presented itself. Certainly they were not models of purity, as their offspring prove. Sadly, poor Eleanor was apparently not trained in the art of dressmaking. On the 1871 census she is listed as a servant and thus did not possess any needlecraft skills that might have provided an income for her and her family when they fell upon hard times.

The 1870s produced sudden, life-changing patterns for Eleanor. On 28 June 1875 her mother died of tuberculosis of the lungs. It was Eleanor, then aged 22, who registered the death. On 5 April 1876 Eleanor's grandmother Amelia died. The cause of death was given as cirrhosis of the liver. Later that same year, on 6 August, Eleanor's younger sister Amelia married Thomas Byford. In effect, Eleanor at this point had lost the three immediate members of her family.

The story moves forward to 1881. On the census for that year Eleanor appears as the wife of William Archer, a chimney sweep. They were lodging at 5 Broom Cottages, Chatham. There seem to be several irregularities in the entry. Their surname appears as Ache instead of Archer, and Eleanor's age as 25; this could be a badly made '28' (her proper age), or Eleanor might have deliberately lowered her age to be closer to that of her husband, then aged 23. Two children are also listed in the household: William, aged 2, and Nelly, aged 1. Nelly's real name was probably Eleanor. Strangely, there is a note on the census form that appears to indicate that the children were adopted. On their birth certificates their surname is recorded as Archer. I cannot find any record of a marriage. Three other children were born to William and Eleanor: Sarah Ann in 1882, Ada in 1884 and Louisa in 1887.

Everything appeared to be going all right until 1889, when Eleanor and her five children entered Medway Union Workhouse. The reason for their admission perhaps dates back to the previous year. On 21 November 1888, William Archer, aged 28, died in Medway Union Workhouse of phthisis pulmonalis (tuberculosis of the lungs) – probably aggravated by his job as a chimney sweep. The reason he died in Medway Union Workhouse may have been that the workhouses often provided a basic infirmary for the poor. Had he been an inmate of the workhouse, his death would most likely have been registered by the master of the workhouse. Instead, the informant is Elizabeth Stevens, William's sister. This simple act raises more questions. Where was Eleanor? Had she parted from William, or was she already in the workhouse? We may never find the answers. It could simply be that William was nursed by his sister while Eleanor struggled to survive with her five children.

What is abundantly clear is that, without their provider, Eleanor and her children were eventually forced into the dreaded and degrading process of going into the workhouse.

The Medway Union Workhouse admission book for 22 May 1889 reads:

Eleanor Hansford, age 33, calling Needlework, religion C of E, born 1856.*

William, her child, age 11, born 1878

Eleanor, her child, age 10, born 1879*

Sarah Ann, her child, age 7, born 1882

Ada, her child, age 5, born 1884

Louisa, her child, age 2, born 1887

Eleanor had by this time reverted to her maiden name, Hansford, which gives more substance to the theory that she was never actually married to William Archer but that they had a common-law arrangement. From this point on, all the family members used the name

---

* These two dates appear to be incorrect. Eleanor was born in 1853 and her daughter Eleanor in 1880.

Hansford, even though the children had been registered on their birth certificates as Archer.

Were the workhouses as bad as is so often assumed? In a word, yes. They were provided by the parish, they cost the parish money, and they were deliberately kept as unpleasant as possible to discourage people from seeking their shelter. There appears to be a common concept at the time that to make the workhouses more agreeable would encourage the lazy and work-shy among the poor to abuse the refuge they provided. It was as if the poor were to be punished for being unable to support themselves and their families. Charles Dickens lived in Chatham as a boy, and it is widely believed that Medway Union Workhouse was the model for the establishment described so vividly in his novel *Oliver Twist*.

The conditions inside the workhouse were harsh and hard. On arrival inmates would be deprived of their own clothing and forced to wear the workhouse garb, often a kind of rough uniform. Men and women were separated. Hair was often cropped, particularly that of the children. The work was strenuous and the hours long. Men were usually given jobs such as chopping firewood, and the women were made to pick oakum, a tedious job consisting of pulling apart the strands of ends of rope for use later in caulking the timbers of wooden ships. This would have been the kind of environment Eleanor encountered when she entered the workhouse.

On 27 August 1889, three months after admission, Eleanor discharged herself and her children. There would have been no opposition from the workhouse authorities.

But Eleanor and her family were soon to be back. Eleanor must have tried desperately to provide a different kind of life for her family, but with no skills, and five children to provide for, the task was almost impossible without family support, and this was clearly not forthcoming. The workhouse was the only solution available to her. The Admissions and Discharges book makes grim reading:

19 September 1889 admittance

7 October 1889 discharge

16 October 1889 admittance

1 September 1890 discharge

From then on life for poor Eleanor was downhill all the way. She appears to have tried to rectify her situation, but each time the odds were stacked against her. The pattern continued, with only a matter of days between discharge and readmission.

It is tempting to wonder what effect this state of affairs must have had on the children. It is possible, but by no means certain, that the eldest had some form of basic education. Conditions in the workhouse were notorious. Inmates were subject to a strict routine of hard work and supervision, and even children were employed on tasks.

On 1 July 1890, Eleanor's daughter Eleanor, then aged 11, was sent by her mother to a

Mrs Stevens at 8 Russell Square in Brook, a village near Chatham. The name Stevens crops up again and again. This could well have been Elizabeth Stevens, William Archer's sister.

Once children had reached a certain age, it was common practice for them to be despatched to employment outside the workhouse. Boys would be placed in paid work or, if they were lucky, apprenticed to learn a trade. Girls would normally be found work as servants. Perhaps Eleanor anticipated this happening and sent her eldest daughter to somebody she knew rather than waiting for the workhouse to act.

There is an entry in the workhouse record for 8 September 1892 that shows William being admitted to the establishment on his own. It is not known whether the rest of the family were inmates at the time.

On 8 October 1894 Eleanor entered the workhouse for the last time. This time she had only three children with her: Sarah, aged 12, Ada, age 10, and Louisa, aged 7. By that time William, her only son, had been sent by the workhouse to a Navy training ship.

On 22 December 1894 Eleanor died in the workhouse. Her age was given as 38, though she would have been slightly older. The cause of death was recorded as phthisis, probably as a result of tuberculosis.

Eleanor's remaining children stayed in the care of the workhouse until they were considered to be of working age. Sarah and Ada were sent into service when they were old enough, while at the time of the 1901 census Louisa, the youngest, aged 13, was still in Medway Union Workhouse, recorded as 'scholar'. Eleanor, the eldest daughter, had two illegitimate daughters baptised in Medway Union Workhouse chapel: Nellie Elizabeth in 1898, and Sarah Ann in 1900. Eleanor married Charles Ernest Stevens in 1902 and apparently went on to have twelve more children.

A tragic story, and one that clearly indicates the hardships and frailty of life in Victorian times. If a person born into poverty could work, it was possible to survive. If it was no longer possible for the head of the household to work, then his or her dependants faced starvation. Their only hope of any assistance from the state was to seek admittance to the workhouse and suffer the humiliation and harshness of life there.

## LILY COLLIER

It is surprising that even in family history research one can spend a considerably amount of time trying to solve a question when the answer is there all the time, staring one in the face. 'Poor research,' I can hear experts muttering. My retort would be, 'Find me a family history researcher who has not experienced the same thing.'

Lily Collier is a perfect example of this. I had carefully written down her name when I compiled the original list based on my father's recollections. My father had been most emphatic about her, even adding as an afterthought, 'We think they went to America,' referring to Lily Collier and her husband. Oh, if only I had asked more questions at the time!

In the early days of my research, I concentrated on building up my family tree, filling in gaps and dates. For the Wigan side of the family things moved quite quickly. I spent hours in the Family Records Centre going through the record books, tracing family members and their offspring. I spent a fortune obtaining copies of certificates and, sad to relate, occasionally ordered the wrong one. But that is a mistake easily made, and the majority of family historians will admit to having done so.

I did my best to find a Lily Collier who would fit into the family. Early on I discovered that Collier is not such an uncommon name, and this hampered my research activities a little. However, try as I might I could not solve the mystery. When I finally did succeed, it was in quite a simple way. My cousin in Wigan still had a few family photographs. I was anxious to obtain at least some copies of these for my own records, as nearly all were connected with my ancestors. Knowing my interest, my cousin very kindly sent me some copies on a CD. It was while I was printing them out that one of them produced the answer I had long sought. I was looking at a photograph of a rather smart young couple; both stared intently at the camera, the man standing and the young woman sitting down: the traditional pose for Victorian photographs. Our Victorian ancestors loved having their photograph taken, and this young couple were no exception. The young man was clearly in his best suit, displaying a watch chain, while the woman wore a jaunty hat and had the required narrow waist of the period. What caught my eye was a brief note made on the heading: 'Auntie Lily and Uncle Jim Collier, sister of grandfather Hansford'.

So there was the answer I had searched for. Lily Collier was one of Thomas Henry's daughters, Elizabeth Reynolds, who married James Collier. I kicked myself for not solving the mystery before, because I had already obtained the marriage certificate for the young couple in the photograph. Why I had not related the woman to Lily Collier I will never know. Clearly either Elizabeth did not like her real name, or her family had adopted for her the nickname Lily. I had simply never associated the two names. Had she been referred to as Liz or Lizzie things would have been simpler from my point of view.

So the mystery of the identity of Lily Collier was cleared up at long last. The loose ends, such as any American connection, were still peppered with further questions. I had glanced through the records for Ellis Island, the arrival point for all immigrants from Europe during the 19th and early-20th centuries. A number of Colliers were listed entering the USA, but I was unable to establish any link to James and Elizabeth (or Lily). An added problem is that to date I had never established whether the couple had any children; that would have been another clue when viewing the Ellis Island records. My cousin Mildred once told me that she had heard of somebody from the family going to America with the intention of sending for the rest of his family as soon as he had established himself. Apparently he disappeared and was never heard of again. Was that James Collier? Somehow I did not think it was, but at that stage I could not be sure. I once heard that we had family in Montana, but the relative who told me this had no further information. It was my hope that the 1911 census would provide further answers. Unfortunately this was not the case, and the whereabouts of this family remained a mystery until quite recently, when a chance find by my cousin revealed strong evidence that James and Lily Collier did indeed go to America, giving credence to the remark made by my father all those years ago. The information gleaned to date is recorded in more detail in the entry in Part 2 of this book dealing with the children of Thomas Henry Hansford and Harriet Eliza Reynolds.

# EXPLORING THE FAMILY LEGENDS

## THE UNCLAIMED FORTUNE

Most families have some story that is passed down from one generation to another. The Hansford family is no exception.

The following story was related to me many years ago by my father, who had been told it by his sisters.

Apparently a distant cousin of the family had discovered by some means that a sum of money left in a will remained unclaimed by eligible members of the family. This cousin had carried out extensive research into the story, believing himself to be a leading candidate to receive the legacy. However, it seemed that one of the requirements for making a claim was to 'prove that a certain Miss Somebody married a certain Mr Somebody in Waterloo parish church, London'. It had become a matter of some urgency by the time he heard about it, because the deadline for making a claim was fast approaching due to the ruling whereby unclaimed money goes to the government after 100 years. However, the enthusiastic search by my distant relative came to a sudden halt when he was told by the vicar of Waterloo parish church that all the church records had been destroyed in the Blitz on London during the Second World War.

When I first heard this story, I had no inkling about family history, how it worked, or what records were available. At the same time it was a fascinating account that gripped my imagination. I kept asking myself questions. Who was the cousin who tried to find the money? How did he find out about the money in the first place? Who were the other people involved? I resolved to find all the answers one day.

Many years were to pass before I had sufficient time to do so. When I began the enormous task of researching my family history, I was at first too busy plotting the family tree, learning about each generation as it appeared. I thought about the story many times, but somehow it always came back to one basic question: how did my relative find out about the legacy? There was simply insufficient information to enable me to pursue the matter.

However, my research revealed some clues. 'Waterloo parish church' had to be the church of St John the Evangelist, which is in Waterloo Road, quite close to the present-day Waterloo railway station. It could not be a coincidence that my great-grandparents had married there. A visit to the church revealed that it had received a direct hit by a bomb on the night of Sunday 8 December 1940. The people sheltering in the crypt had emerged unscathed, but the building had been completely burnt out. It was not until 1951 that the restoration was completed, and the church rededicated by the then Princess Elizabeth and the Archbishop of Canterbury.

These findings gave some substance to the story, but I was still a long way from finding the full details or a logical starting point.

More information came to light eventually in rather a strange way. Through my family history research I had renewed acquaintance with cousins on my father's side of the family. They were interested in my research, but were unable to offer a great deal of factual knowledge other than odd snippets of information that came to light as we chatted. Very often these did not reveal themselves as being of value to my cousins, but for me they might prove to be the starting point for something exciting. It was one of these comments that put me on the right track regarding the missing money. During a telephone conversation, when we were casually talking about the unclaimed money and who tried to claim it, my cousin remarked, 'Perhaps it was Harry Fair.' At that point I had not heard of Harry Fair, but further investigation revealed that his mother was Thomas Henry's daughter Fanny, who had married a member of the Fair family in 1904. This gave a direct link back to St John the Evangelist church and Thomas Henry and Harriet Eliza's marriage in 1850.

So the leading player in the mystery could be Harry Fair, but that still left the biggest question unanswered. How did he know about the existence of the money? Help was to come some months later, again from one of my cousins. I was making one of my regular Sunday afternoon telephone calls to my eldest cousin, Mildred, and was as usual alert to any bit of information I might be able to glean relating to family history. I happened to bring up the question of Harry Fair and the elusive money. I remarked casually that I would like to know where Harry Fair had found out about it in the first instance. Mildred replied, 'He saw it in the *News of the World*; they used to have an unclaimed money section.' I could not let this pass without pressing her for more details. 'It must have been after the war,' I persisted, with the thought of Harry Fair's meeting with the vicar of St John's and the war damage to the church in mind. 'No,' said Mildred. 'It must have been in 1939.' How she knew this I did not question, but she was quite definite about the year.

At last I had a definite clue to follow up. Within a few days I made the journey to the British Library's newspaper archive in Colindale, North London, housed in an impressive purpose-built facility erected in the 1930s. After going through the formality of obtaining a reader's ticket and waiting about half an hour for my order to be processed, I was at last given the reel of film covering the *News of the World* for 1939.

Seated in the gloom of the reading room, with most of the surrounding light coming from the film reader on which I was concentrating, I slowly made my way through each week of the year. It was time-consuming work, but after a while I grew quite adept at finding the page in each edition that included the unclaimed money column.

In the newspaper for Sunday 5 March 1939 I found the following entry: 'Amelia Seymour, late of Bognor Regis, died 9 November 1938.'

The name Seymour meant nothing to me: to my knowledge I had no ancestors or relatives of that name. What was of interest, though, was the list of people her estate was to be divided between. It contained four Hansfords, but none of the names were familiar to me. From the notice it was clear that the solicitor appointed to deal with the will was having problems tracing some of the people on the list. It looked as if Amelia Seymour was a spinster or a widow who had no close kin so had named all these distant relatives in her will. Some she had obviously had no contact with for some considerable time, because the list was peppered with comments such as 'believed died' or 'some time of'.

The same notice appeared again in the *News of the World* on 2 April and 16 April 1939.

I could not help experiencing a tremor of excitement at finding this entry. I had a hunch that this was the notice Harry Fair had seen. However, just to be on the safe side I decided to go through the years preceding and following 1939. In the end I looked at every issue of the *News of the World* from 1935 to 1955, which required numerous visits to Colindale. No further information of any interest came to light. In fact I only came across one other entry for the name Hansford, and that one was clearly not relevant.

I felt that this discovery demanded further investigation. It seemed a logical next step to obtain a copy of Amelia Seymour's will and see if this revealed any further clues. This meant a visit to the Probate Search Room in High Holborn, a rather inconspicuous building requiring entry through an airport-type security system. Once I was inside, checking and identifying the will was a comparatively simple task. There are rows of books for every year since 1858, with one book for each year. Details of the deceased and his or her will are listed alphabetically. It did not take me long to find the will for Amelia Seymour in the book for 1939 and order a copy at the counter for the grand sum of £5.

Unfortunately, the eagerly awaited arrival of this document in the post a few days later did not justify my enthusiasm, for the details it contained did not throw any further light on the subject. It looked to me as if the instructions in the will had been carried out by the executors, and the total estate did not amount to an excessive sum, even by 1939 standards.

So my research into the mysterious legacy seemed to have come to rather an abrupt end. I continued to make enquiries, asking more knowledgeable people whenever I had the opportunity. On one occasion I had the good fortune to speak with a helpful member of staff at the Court Funds Division in London, who expressed the opinion that any further research would be beset with even greater problems. As he tactfully explained, they themselves had difficulty in tracing wills and money only ten years old, let alone seventy. It seemed but a slim chance that any records would be available from the Chichester solicitor mentioned in Amelia's will, though I did find out later that the practice was still in existence at the same address.

Though the story now has a great deal more substance to it, it remains incomplete without the final chapter. However, having spent a good deal of time and effort on this tiny fragment of my family's history, I did begin to draw some conclusions about it.

It seems fair to assume that like many legends the story grew with each telling and that bits of its contents became enlarged over the years. It could well be that Harry Fair, reading his Sunday paper one day in 1939, came across the same notice in the unclaimed money column that I was to read all these years later. Perhaps it was a regular habit of his to glance at it, as many people do. He would have been immediately attracted to this particular entry when he saw the name Hansford, because he would no doubt have known that it was his mother's maiden name. He would also have known that the family originally came from the south of England. He might also have known that his grandmother Harriet Eliza was married in St John the Evangelist church in London. These facts could well have been the prompting he needed to follow up the newspaper notice. With no previous knowledge and with no interest other than in the advertised legacy, Harry Fair may have thought that the most logical action to take would be to visit the church where his grandmother had married, to obtain documented evidence.

There are of course major flaws in the original story. Even if the records of the church had been burnt, alternative ones would have been available elsewhere. I have myself looked at them many times in the London Metropolitan Archives. It seems odd that even with limited knowledge, Harry Fair did not know this or find out in the course of his enquiries. In fairness, though, it has to be remembered that this was a time well before the emergence of family history as a popular hobby with an abundance of records freely available. When Harry Fair carried out his investigation, genealogy was a specialised field, and considerable effort and dedication were required to locate records.

Another odd detail is the length of time involved in the search. Harry Fair saw the notice in March 1939. The Second World War did not begin until September of that year. Given the obvious urgency involved, it seems strange that he did not commence research straight away. The fact that he was told the records had been burnt indicates that he visited the church after it reopened in April 1951. It does not seem feasible that he would visit a burnt-out shell, though of course it is possible that he did so and was directed to the appropriate church authorities.

There is also the question of the unclaimed money. I have never discovered any ruling that money has to be claimed within a certain time. My finding has been that if money remains unclaimed it goes into a court-held fund. Any person who believes that he or she has a legal right to the money and can provide the required evidence can at any time make a claim to it. Records of these funds are maintained, but it is a complex operation to research them without specific knowledge of a particular legacy.

Out of interest, I did some research into the Hansfords listed in the will, but I could find no evidence of any link with my family.

In conclusion, it would appear that unless further information comes to light, the current pattern of research must end where it is for the present. I am sceptical that any further research is possible or would yield more details. There appears to be nobody available today who can confirm or refute the story and fill in the missing bits, so sadly it looks as if it will pass into history as an unsolved mystery.

**THE MISSING SAILOR**

This tale has always intrigued me. I think a great deal of my interest in it stems from the fact that it was this story that cemented my interest in family history firmly into place.

As previously mentioned, my father had told me that our ancestors had travelled north from Kent to Wigan, his place of birth, because of a tragic incident at sea that had taken the lives of several brothers. I knew there must be more to the story. I had visions of my ancestors being wealthy ship owners or at least ship's captains or mates. I imagined them sailing across the seas in magnificent clipper ships, reaping the rewards of rich cargos.

It is always a little disappointing to have such illusions rudely shattered when one gets down to the real work of research. It did not take me long to establish that my father's story had many flaws in it, even if there was some truth along the way. The first thing I discovered was that the person who had made the trek to Wigan with his family was not James Hansford at all, but his son Thomas Henry. James was indeed a sailor, but he served in the Royal Navy, not in the merchant fleet.

Although Thomas Henry Hansford was educated at the Greenwich Royal Hospital School, he was never sent to sea from there as was quite common. Instead he became a whitesmith

– a person who worked in tin or an early form of galvanised metal.

So all this documented information tends to blow apart the original account. In my experience such stories do usually have some element of truth in them, but in this particular case it has been extremely difficult to find, as these events happened such a long time ago and perhaps went unrecorded for subsequent generations other than by word of mouth – and this is how the distortion takes place. It is rather like the party game where one person whispers something to the person sitting next to them, who in turn passes it on to the next person, and so on. By the time those few words have gone round the room, the original will often have changed out of all recognition, providing great hilarity. Unless family stories are supported with documented evidence of what actually took place, they become distorted with retelling and time, because each person relating it colours it with his or her own thinking.

While it is not good practice in any research to base conclusions on speculation about what might have happened or to merely offer up undocumented hearsay as a means of solving a mystery, it does happen that the researcher during long hours of searching begins to form certain ideas of what might be the origin of a story and to offer them up for consideration.

This is the situation I have reached regarding this interesting but elusive story. As the basic elements of the original story were shown to be incorrect in the early days of research, I have had to delve deeper for clues that may provide the answer. Clearly the key must lie with Thomas Henry. We know that his father died when he was very young, so that tends to eliminate him from the picture.

Thomas Henry had an older brother, John James Colliver, who disappeared from the records in about 1839, when he would have been about 11 or 12 years old. I have always thought it rather strange that an application was made by the boys' mother for Thomas Henry to be admitted to Greenwich School, but not for his older brother. Did this mean that he was already engaged in some form of career? I believe the answer is yes. For a young boy living in Chatham, with its strong maritime connection, it would have been quite easy to go off to sea, even at such an early age. Even naval ships would employ young boys as 'powder monkeys' to carry the kegs of gunpowder from the magazine to the gun decks. Merchant ships very often included a cabin boy in the crew, to perform the domestic drudgery. I think it is highly likely that this was the reason that I have been unable to find any further trace of John. Was he the person behind the original story? Was he lost at sea? It is possible, but since Thomas Henry did not move to Wigan until a good thirty-five years after his brother's disappearance from the records, it is perhaps not so likely, unless they kept in touch with each other, which would have been difficult if John was away at sea.

There is another possibility. Thomas Henry had a son, also named Thomas Henry, who was born in Greenwich in 1852, the first child of the marriage. He appears on the 1861 census but not on the one for 1871. My father once remarked, 'We think he went to Australia.' Was this the answer? Did he decide to go to Australia as a teenager? Early in my research I felt that there was a strong possibility that this son of Thomas Henry was the link to the story. It seemed plausible that as a young, headstrong teenager he had run off to sea. This theory led me to wonder whether he had drowned. Any attempt to address this speculation was dogged by obstacles. Trying to find a missing person lost at sea is extremely difficult without knowing the name of the vessel involved or the date. Staff at record offices shook their heads when I confronted them with the questions I wanted answers to. Unless I had more information, they told me, the task was virtually impossible.

Thomas Henry's disappearance dogged me for years. I continued with other research, but always the unanswered question lurked in the background. Recent research has provided sufficient evidence to indicate that he did emigrate, to either Australia or New Zealand, so that eliminates the theory that he was the family member lost at sea. However, it is still possible that this event was one of the reasons for the move to the north of England. In one sense Thomas Henry would have effectively been lost to the family, as moving to the other side of the world in the 19th century was not the simple excursion it is today: it involved a long and often dangerous voyage, and it is extremely doubtful that he communicated with his family again once he arrived in the new land. The postal service was in its infancy and there were no telephones in those days. With no word from his eldest son, and with his other sons growing up, Thomas Henry may well have felt that the time was right to move away from the coast, before any of his other sons got similar ideas of emigrating or of seeking a living from the sea.

There is another facet of the story related by my father. He had quite firmly indicated that 'more than one brother' had been lost at sea. This raises another intriguing question. As related elsewhere, Thomas Henry's sister Eliza appears to have given birth to an illegitimate son, John James, in 1850. Apart from his birth certificate, I have been unable to find any record of him. He would have been roughly the same age as his cousin Thomas Henry. Did the two boys run off together to sea and thus account for the plural aspect of the story? It is an interesting theory, but no evidence has so far emerged to support it.

There is another possible reason for the move to Wigan. According to the brief details on the census returns, Thomas Henry was an engineer in later life. He was a journeyman: that is, he was not permanently employed in one place, but went from location to location wherever work might be found. Documentary evidence shows that the family probably moved to Wigan between 1874 and 1879. This was a boom time for the cotton mills in Lancashire. People were coming from all over England to the prosperous north in search of work and the security it afforded. I think this was part of the reason for Thomas Henry's move. The loss of a brother or a son might have been involved in his decision, but I think the real reason has been lost in the retelling of the story over the years.

Can any more be found out? At this stage it seems extremely unlikely. There is still the Australian angle to explore in depth. However, the search for anyone lost at sea is beset with problems, unless one is in possession of the name of the vessel. This is particularly the case with merchant ships, whose records of crew members or passengers are not so readily available. There are no longer any aged members of the family who might just give that little clue needed. It is possible that the whole story will remain just another unsolved loose end of family history.

# REFLECTION

When I first started researching my family history I had only a vague idea of what I would be able to find. In my ignorance, I suppose I imagined that all that was necessary was to go to the various record offices, quickly look up the information and build up a history of my family without too much trouble. Even the various family legends could, I felt sure, be resolved with time and patience.

One of the things I had not envisaged was that it would take me ten years' hard work just to reach the stage where I am now. Even now I do not consider the job fully completed; the research will continue, albeit perhaps at a lower intensity. Somebody once said to me that family history is never completed, and that is true: there is always some further bit of information that suddenly appears out of the blue.

In terms of family history research, ten years is not a long time. I have met other people who have been at the task for twenty or thirty years. At the other end of the scale, I have also encountered people who claim to have completed the task in a matter of a few days, using the internet. I am tempted to ask what sort of research they have done. It is very easy to pluck a likely-looking person from a list on a website and claim him or her as an ancestor. The internet is a very useful tool for family history researchers, but finds have to be treated with caution – and checked against official records. I have come across research by other people into my ancestors that I know to be inaccurate. Statements have been made that I have demonstrated to be totally incorrect.

Family history has reached all-time popularity. Television programmes such as *Who Do You Think You Are?* have contributed to this rising interest. Such programmes have given some people the idea that family history is easy: that all one has to do is to go to a record office and after a little searching walk out with results. Oh, if only it were like that! Most researchers will vouch for often spending hours and hours searching, with little to show for it at the end.

What the novice family history researcher should also be aware of is the fact that television programmes like *Who Do You Think You Are?* are made for entertainment; the subject involved will have been selected because there is a background of ancestors that will provide an interesting programme. Not every family history researcher will discover that his or her ancestors were famous or were connected with some well-known bit of history. The majority will find that their ancestors lived quite ordinary lives, did their best to provide for their families, no doubt grumbled at the same things as we do and faced life's problems as best they could. Most lived in obscurity, except for a record in their local church register. Only occasionally did their job make them famous or provide a record in a dusty book somewhere, waiting for family historians to find generations later.

I consider myself extremely lucky that I have ancestors who served in the Royal Navy. Without that advantage the whole job of research would have been much harder and I would not be in the position I am in today. It is thanks to my great-great-great- grandfather James Hansford completing his twenty-seven years in the service and then clearly encouraging his sons to enlist that I was provided with a framework on which to build. The achievement of that momentous day when, seated in the quiet atmosphere of the reading room at the National Archives, I lifted the lid on three generations of my ancestors, opened the door to a hitherto unknown part of my family's history. I had previously had no inkling of any Royal Navy connection; I do not believe my father knew about it, either. I suspect even my grandfather may not have known the details, or if he did, perhaps he did not talk about it. Thomas Henry Hansford died over 100 years ago, and with him quite possibly passed the truth about the history of my family. If the suggestion that he moved to Wigan to separate his family from the sea is correct, then in that objective he succeeded.

### LOOSE ENDS

It is an inevitable part of family history research that along the way one comes across ancestors who apparently disappear from the records. One can expect to experience problems finding ancestors prior to the advent of compulsory registration in 1837, but when the search falls within the period of official records the situation becomes both puzzling and trying. Sometimes the answer turns out to be a simple case of the record being under a different name by error. This was the case of John James, one of Thomas Henry Hansford's sons. I spent a few years searching for him and wasted money purchasing two incorrect death certificates before finding him by accident while I was looking for something else. The reason I had not found him previously? He died in a location where I did not expect to find him, and his name was spelt incorrectly. Only from other details on the death certificate could I be sure I had found the right person.

I have several of these loose ends, as I term them: ancestors who just do not want to be found. I have not so far managed to find the birth of Harriet Eliza Reynolds, and much remains hidden concerning her son Thomas Henry Hansford, who, as mentioned previously, apparently emigrated to Australia. There are a few other missing ancestors, including John James, Thomas Henry's sister Eliza's illegitimate son. It looks as if Eliza got married in 1852, but after that she also seems to have disappeared. This could be a simple case of the name on the census differing slightly from the one being searched. The census records are a marvellous tool for family historians, but an error in recording or transcribing can mean that an elusive ancestor remains hidden.

The missing ancestors on the male line are the ones that are of prime importance to me, because they carry forward the Hansford name. I have as a matter of routine carried out basic research into the various daughters who have married and changed their names, but I have only carried out deeper research into the female side when there is a direct ancestor involved, such as my grandmother Mary Worthington. In family history it is quite easy to get carried away and find oneself researching on several fronts, which can distract from the main focus. Some of the female line looks quite an interesting and satisfying area of research for the future.

## THE ROAD AHEAD

The decision to write up and publish my findings was not taken lightly. There are some areas of research that still require attention.

I hesitated to commit the research to paper, thinking that as soon as things were written up fresh evidence might appear that could provide answers to some of the outstanding questions. There is always the possibility that tomorrow there will be a breakthrough. I think it is this optimism that keeps the dedicated family history researcher going.

However, at this stage little would be achieved by delaying the process. There will be nothing more to add to the greater part of my research, for the simple reason that there appears to be very little more to find out. I am convinced that the few snippets that may subsequently come to light will not substantially alter the whole and will serve only to embellish the research that has already taken place.

In my opinion, the greatest area of unanswered questions lies in the Australian connection. Information received from Australia in the course of my research suggests that Thomas Henry Hansford junior, who emigrated there, married twice, the first time in New Zealand. This opens up a completely new line of investigation. The fresh questions to answer are numerous, perhaps the most important being how or why Thomas Henry came to be in New Zealand.

Initial research has not provided any answers, and as I write it looks as if further progress may take some time. However, I am satisfied that the basic work to establish what happened to Thomas Henry once he disappeared from the UK records has been completed.

Other areas of research still outstanding are on the whole less important. The majority have already had some work carried out on them and so far this has turned up little new information. In a few cases I do not believe anything more can be achieved at this stage. Most relate to male heirs who have disappeared from the records. The most prominent ancestors to achieve the status of 'missing persons' are these:

William Hansford, son of James Hansford senior: no trace after about 1839.

John James Colliver Hansford, eldest son of James Hansford junior: no trace after around 1838/1839.

John James Hansford, son of Eliza Hansford, Thomas Henry's sister: born in 1850 and no trace after that date.

There are a few other intriguing lines of enquiry that have been followed up over the years, but investigations so far have not revealed any new evidence of the individuals in question being distant ancestors; nevertheless, they are still open for research. One of these is a James Hansford who mysteriously appeared in the 1870s. I discovered him first on the birth certificate of a woman named Maud Alice Hansford. In spite of trying every angle I can think of, I have still not been able to find out any more about him. At first I had high hopes that I had discovered Eliza's illegitimate son John James, but without more information I cannot be sure. I could be completely wrong. Maud Alice's mother's surname is Jones. Not an easy name to follow up!

It is a facet of family history that very often names crop up that look like those of possible family ancestors but turn out after a good deal of research to be somebody else's family.

A typical example is a William Hansford I came across in the naval records. At first I was over the moon, thinking I had discovered James senior's son, another elusive member of my family. From the naval records everything looked good. His age was the same; his entry into the service was about right. However, he consistently gave his county of birth as Sussex. I did a lot of research into his naval career and then came to the conclusion that I could be wrong about his being my ancestor. A confirmation of birth would provide the answer, but so far I have not been able to find one in the parish records.

These loose ends are one of the reasons that in the opening chapters I described these documents as being presented as 'work in hand', but that statement should not distract from the scope and value of the work already carried out and now presented as a factual and documented account of the history of my branch of the Hansford family tree.

# PART 2

# THE HANSFORD FAMILY 1770-1904

c (circa) = Baptism or estimated date of Birth

James Hansford
c1770-1845
=
Elizabeth Colliver
c1772-1840
m 1796 Fowey, Cornwall.

John
c1798-1829
=
Elizabeth Saxby
m 1829 Rochester, Kent.

James
c1802-33
=
Eliza Spencelayh
c1806-38
m 1824 Frindsbury, Kent.

Elizabeth
c1805-?

Mary Ann
1807-?
=
James Carnell
m 1824 Frindsbury, Kent.

Amelia
1809-76

Elizabeth
1811-13

Caroline
c1814-?
=
Charles Thomas Fransom
m 1839 Chatham, Kent.

William
c1816-?

Samuel
1819-69

Amelia Elizabeth
c1830-?
=
Charles Goff
m 1853 Chatham, Kent.

John James Colliver
c1828-?

Thomas Henry
1830 1903
=
Harriet Eliza Reynolds
c1832-1913
m 1850 Lambeth, London.

Eliza Ann
c1832-?
- - - - - - - - - - -
William Witmore
m 1852 Chatham, Kent.

John James Hansford

Amelia Elizabeth
1850-?

Amelia Elizabeth
c1830 /?5

Amelia Elizabeth
1855-?
=
Thomas William Byford
m 1876 Chatham, Kent.

Eleanor Elizabeth
1853-94

Louisa
1887-?
=
Henry John Daley
m 1911 Chatham, Kent.

William
1878-1918
=
Louisa Ellen Olivia Daley
m 1909 Chatham, Kent.

Eleanor Elizabeth
1880-?

Sarah Ann
1882-?

Ada
1884-?

Thomas Henry
1852-1931
1) Mary Ann Clarke
c1846-1906
m c1874 New Zealand or Australia
2) Annie Sawyer
1879-1959
m 1910 Melbourne, Aus.

Elizabeth Ann
1855-58

Mary Ann Eliza
1857-?
=
John Jones
m 1883 Wigan, Lancs.

William Charles
1858-1965
=
Mary Worthington
1861-1932
m 1885 Wigan, Lancs.

Caroline Elizabeth
1860-79

Charles Saunders
1862 1940
=
Eliza Storey
1864-1928
m 1887 Bolton, Lancs.

James John
1864-1923

Elizabeth Reynolds
1866-?

James Collier
1866-?
m 1889 Wigan, Lancs.

Frederick Edwin
1869-1923
=
Mary Alice Challender
m 1914 Westhoughton, Lancs.

Fanny Ada Charlotte
1870-1930

Henry Fair
c1868-?
m 1904 Wigan, Lancs.

Harriet Georgina
1872-?
1) William Warden
c1864-1911
m 1895 Wigan, Lancs.
2) James Collier
m 1921 St. Louis, USA.

George Wilfred
1918 34

Caroline
1886-1969

George
1889-1974
=
Edith Crichley
m 1917 Wigan, Lancs.

Mary
1892-1968
=
Alfred Carter
1891-1956
m 1921 Wigan, Lancs.

Nellie
1895-96

Thomas
1898-1965
=
Mildred Hutchinson
1896-1971
m 1925 Oulton, Yorkshire.

Annie
1901-72
=
Horace Grounds Bannister
1894-1987
m 1939 Wigan, Lancs.

Lily
1904-91

Violet
1887-1963

Harry
1888-1948
=
Emily Mary Hore
m 1920 Manchester.

Harriet Eliza
1890-?
Wilfred Mayoh
m 1914 Blackpool, Lancs.

Henrietta Frances May
1895-1923

# JAMES HANSFORD (SENIOR) 1770-1845

I begin with James because he is the first member of the family for whom I have definite documented evidence, and this is mainly due to the availability of meticulous naval records. However, because he was born in the 18th century, details of his birth and marriage are not so easy to establish. UK research from 1837 onwards is assisted by the availability of birth, marriage and death certificates, which provide the details needed for identification of the individual concerned, such as place of birth, parents and age. However, research into records prior to civil registration has to be carried out using parish (church) registers, and these can present continuity problems. Minimum details listed, similar names, and damaged or faded documents all make family history research prior to 1837 more challenging.

From naval records over a period of 20 years, I was able to pinpoint James's birth year as 1770. The records are fairly consistent on this point. His place of birth is slightly more ambiguous. In his naval records it appears variously as Dorsetshire, Bridport and Litton. The only possible baptism listed for a James Hansford was recorded in the village of Swyre on 18 February 1770. Litton can be no other than Litton Cheney, which is only a short distance from Swyre. It is when I looked into who James's parents were that I encountered some of the problems mentioned above. The entry for James's baptism in the parish register for Swyre simply reads, 'Jas, son of William and Tomasin Hansford'. The only likely marriage that ties up with this birth is again listed in Swyre, on 2 January 1768.[1] The entry reads: 'William Hansford of Askerswell married Frances Tibby of this parish' (Swyre). If this marriage is accepted as being that of James's parents, there is confusion between the two names given for James's mother/William's wife. Tomasin is the female equivalent of Thomas and is not in common use today. Was Tomasin a nickname Frances was known by locally, even to the parson? There is ample evidence to indicate that this particular parson was not inclined to go into detail. Other entries in the register are equally brief.

It was thanks to an excellent piece of research by Michael Hansford that a breakthrough came. Every parson was obliged every three months to forward to his bishop copies of the register, known as Bishops' Transcripts. These usually contain similar details to the register; however, there can be variations, and this was the case with James's baptismal entry, which reads 'James Hansford, son of William and Frances his wife'. The wife's name is somewhat indistinct, but can just be made out. The parson may have felt that he needed to be more precise in the names he wrote on a document for his bishop, and hence declined the use of the name Tomasin in favour of the correct name, Frances. While a slight element of doubt may exist regarding James's parents and birth, I am convinced that the information unearthed does relate to James, for the simple reason that there is no record of any other likely birth in Dorset at the time. I think we are just dealing with the vagueness of the times and the fact that the parish records were never intended for family history research.

After the birth of their son, William and Frances seemed to completely disappear. Nor did James appear to have had any brothers and sisters. Even his mother is a mystery: though it would seem she was from the parish of Litton Cheney or Swyre, there does not appear to be a record of a family of that name in that area, or of any similar name such as Tibbs or Tibbly. It is something that is difficult to explain without the aid of some form of documented evidence. This was a time when someone could disappear and his or her death go unrecorded. It is not unusual to come across a burial entry in a church register for this period for a 'man [or woman] unknown', a situation where the parson has given a Christian burial to the body of some unfortunate man or woman found somewhere. An individual could also be lost at sea with no trace or record. However, the situation is a little more complex when two people are involved. It is still possible that the answer may appear in future research, but so far extensive searching of the documents available has not revealed an explanation. It is possible that one partner of the marriage died and the survivor remarried, the details obscured in other records. For the present it remains a mystery unsolved.

This does of course mean that we have little information about James's early life. It is quite possible that he went to sea as a boy. Swyre and Litton Cheney are not far inland, and at that time nearby Bridport was a thriving fishing port.

From existing documents, we know that in 1788, at the age of 18, James joined HMS *Sprightly*, a 10-gun cutter. At this period of naval history, for ordinary seamen there was no such thing as 'joining the navy'. They were signed on by a ship for the duration of a voyage, however long that might be. At the end of the voyage they were paid off. It was a system whereby seamen were free to serve on either naval ships or the merchant fleet. However, it is surprising how many, once they had served on naval vessels, opted to continue, some remaining on the same ship for a number of voyages. Perhaps conditions on the naval ships were better.

Was life on these ships as bad as we are led to believe? Perhaps by today's standards the answer is yes. Cold and wet for days at a time, cramped living conditions and harsh discipline could be expected. However, working conditions on land were little better in many cases, particularly in the cities or on the land, where many workers had a near-starvation diet, often existing on a day-to-day pittance. Seamen on naval vessels, by contrast, had a diet controlled by regulations. They ate meat several times a week, something many land-based workers could not afford, and they received regular if not generous pay.

When James entered the service of His Majesty, he enlisted as an able seaman, which meant that he already had several years' experience of seamanship. He knew the ropes, literally. From then on he served on a number of ships, usually staying with each for one or two years, although when he joined the *Sans Pareil,* a French ship captured in 1794, he was part of her company for almost five years. He appears to have been regarded as a good, reliable seaman, being listed as the 'Captains Cox'n'[2] on one occasion. James was still serving on the *Sans Pareil* when he met and married Elizabeth Colliver in Fowey, Cornwall.

Elizabeth was the youngest daughter of Thomas Colliver, a cooper by trade; this was a skilled occupation, making wooden barrels and casks. Two of her four sisters had already married seamen from the Royal Navy.

In James's time Fowey was not the idyllic little town popular with holidaymakers that it is today. As well as being an important seaport in the region visited by ships from other countries, it was also frequently used by naval vessels as an anchorage, which accounts for James's presence there and his marriage to Elizabeth Colliver on 23 October 1796 at the parish church of St Fimbarrus.

The lives of sailors' wives were quite hard and lonely in those days. Their menfolk were often away from home for long periods and there would be no communication from them until their ships returned safely to port again. No mobile phones in those days! There is little doubt that there would have been a good deal of companionship between the women, who would support each other as best they could while their men were away sailing the seas and earning money. We can only imagine the relief and excitement when it was announced that a husband's ship was returning to port. Elizabeth may have fared better than many. For most of his career, James appears to have been in the Channel Fleet, which means that his voyages would have been relatively short, as his ships patrolled up and down the English Channel looking after the country's interests.

James and Elizabeth's first child, John, was baptised in Fowey in 1798, followed by James, my great-great-grandfather, in 1802, and Elizabeth, their first daughter, in 1805. Nine children in all were recorded, though two of them did not survive into adulthood.

In 1801 James was promoted to the rank of boatswain. From now on he had warrant officer status. He would have been addressed as 'Mr Hansford' on board ship and would have had a very responsible position in the running of the vessel.

What exactly was the role of a boatswain (pronounced 'bosun')? His main job was to ensure that all the ship's rigging and sails were maintained in first-class working order. He would have had one or more assistants to help him carry out the task, and his job would have been largely supervisory. Another very important job for a boatswain was to use the 'bosun's call' or whistle to issue commands. The whistle would be worn around his neck, almost as a badge of office, and by varying the tone he would use it to alert the crew to the different jobs to be carried out. A perk of his position would be that he might have his own cabin, though it would be small and most likely filled with the materials of his job, such as ropes and other equipment. One of the requirements of the navy was that the person selected for the job of boatswain be of sufficient education to maintain accounts and submit reports. Illiterate boatswains were extremely rare. It would have been difficult to do the job without these basic qualifications, as the navy insisted on accurate and detailed descriptions of where the materials they issued went. It seems, then, that James must have had some ability to read and write.

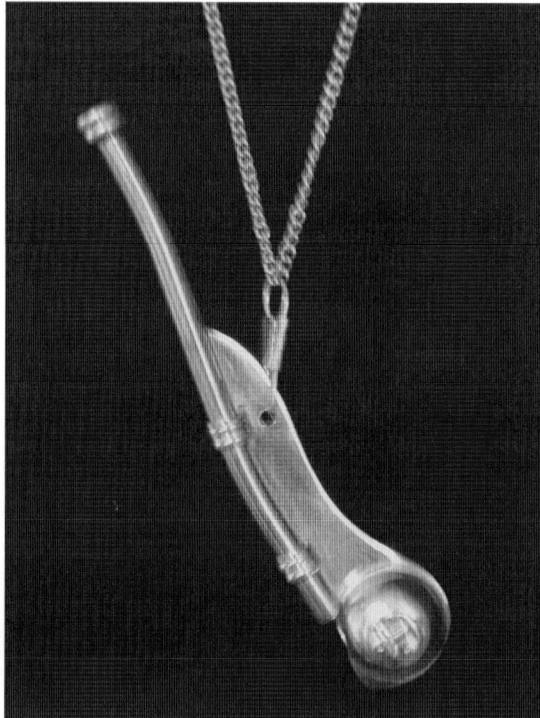

*The Bosun's call*

Sometime between the years 1805 and 1807 James moved his family from Fowey to Portsea. We can determine the time from the baptisms of two of his daughters, one in each town. This move raises an interesting question: how did the family travel to Portsea? The railway network had not yet been developed, and stagecoaches were expensive, even for the gentry. Sea travel seems to have been the most likely, but certainly not on a naval ship. It is a well-known secret that there were often a few women on naval ships; in fact, most captains were aware of the situation and turned a blind eye, provided that it did not get out of hand. (In fact the popular saying 'Show a leg' dates from this period. When the crew were woken up from slumber for duty, the cry 'Show a leg' would sound in the gunroom. Seamen were required to jump out of their hammocks for duty. If a shapely female leg was displayed from a hammock, its owner was left alone until the call came for hammock storage.) Some boatswains did have their wives with them; this was quietly tolerated by some captains, even if it was against the regulations. However, in the case of a woman such as Elizabeth, with three small children – never.

The most likely answer to the question of how James's family travelled from Fowey to Portsea is one suggested by a naval historian at Chatham Dockyard Historical Society. Fowey was a busy port. James and his wife would have known shipping owners or captains, or their agents. With a little tact and patience, James would have been able to secure a passage for his family along the coast to Portsea. The captain or owner of a merchant ship sailing in the right direction would have been willing to earn a little extra income in return for the use of the ship's cabin for a night or two.

Little is known about the family's life in Portsea. The movement of naval families was not as common as might be expected. For the most part, wives remained in one place and brought up the many children conceived when their husbands were home. Clearly James must have had a good reason for moving his family. It may well have been that he was now spending more and more time in the Portsmouth area. Boatswains, like gunners and carpenters, were known as standing officers. They were appointed to a ship and remained with that ship even when it was in dock. Most ships had a home port they returned to from time to time. James may well have been with a ship based in Portsmouth. He may have known that he was unlikely to return to Cornish waters again, so moving his family was a logical step. One can only marvel at the courage and fortitude of Elizabeth in leaving her family and making such a move into the unknown with several small children to look after.

The baptism records of a further three daughters confirm that the family remained in the Portsea area until at least 1811.

Sometime after that date another move was made, this time to Chatham, thereby establishing the family link with that town. It is possible that James employed the same method to move his now enlarged family as he had used on the previous move to Portsea. This move may have been determined by the fact that James was now 'in ordinary'. In peacetime not so many ships were required at sea as during times of conflict, but they had to be maintained in a state of readiness in case they were needed. Of the warrant officers, the purser, boatswain, gunner and carpenter remained on board, together with the cook and a small team of assistants, to carry out the task of keeping the ship in 'running order'. The warrant officers involved in this routine were referred to as being 'in ordinary'.

The precise date of the family's move to Chatham is not known. The family were certainly there in 1813, because the death of their youngest daughter, Elizabeth, was recorded there in that year.

For the rest of his naval career, James appears to have served on ships based at Chatham. He was in ordinary for the last seven years of his service, which would mean that his family saw a great deal more of him. He would have been based at Chatham dockyard, a twenty-minute walk from the town, and would most likely have made the journey many times, dressed in his boatswain's uniform of white trousers and navy-blue jacket and hat. On the way, he would have passed the parish church of St Mary's, where his children were baptised and buried.

What sort of a man would James have been? By today's standards, probably quite a hard character. He had to be because of the job he did. He would certainly not have been the most popular man on board ship. Scarcely a day would have gone by when somebody did not criticise him behind his back or curse him under their breath. James may have administered the punishment of flogging. The task was usually carried out by the assistant boatswain, a rank he might have held at some point in his career.

Now that they had moved for a second time, the family seem to have settled down into Chatham life. Chatham in those days was a very different town from the one it is today, and certainly not like its close neighbour Rochester, which was considered a much nicer place to live. The massive ship-building programme of the Admiralty had resulted in Chatham dockyard expanding rapidly. This meant a huge increase in the town's population as navy personnel and workers took up residence. Chatham was also an army base, and a sizeable quantity of soldiers were garrisoned there. This situation led to an increase in drinking taverns, drunkenness and prostitution. The town's sewerage system did not grow at the same pace as the town itself, leading to ill health, and at least two outbreaks of cholera occurred there. Despite all these problems, people like James and Elizabeth lived and brought up their children in this environment. Two more sons and a daughter were born in Chatham: Caroline in 1814, William in 1816 and Samuel in 1819.

James appears to have been very keen to obtain places in Greenwich Royal Hospital

School for several members of his family. The school was usually reserved for orphaned sons and daughters of naval officers and ratings or for children from naval families that had fallen on hard times. Perhaps James felt that as a warrant officer he had some privilege. Whatever the reason, applications are on record for his children Caroline, James, Samuel and William. It is not know whether the applications for all the children were successful, because the records no longer exist; however, there is strong evidence that James went to the school, and there are documents available to prove that William's application was also successful.

In 1816 James's service in the Royal Navy came to an end. His discharge paper reads

> *May 10th 1816*
> *Chatham. James Hansford in Ordinary*
> *Age 48 Time in HMS 28 [years]*
>
> *Unfit for service due to severe attacks of Rheumatism which he has been invalided on board the Leviathan in June 1794 and Sans Pareil 23 June 1795. In Ordinary 7 years producing the usual certificate.*
>
> *Character and Conduct since being in Ordinary good.*
> (ADM11/36)

From the above document it would appear that poor James suffered for some years from the complaint that ultimately dictated his retirement, a legacy of the cold and wet conditions on board ship.

As a warrant officer, James was lucky enough to receive a pension for the rest of his life. Records indicate that this was £40 per annum. While not a large sum, it was considerably more than most people had to live on in retirement. Retired sailors were free to have a job as well as receiving their naval pension, and many did this to supplement their income. It is quite possible that James did so. Chatham dockyard was close at hand and a man of James's experience would have been a welcome addition to the workforce.

One record during the family's stay in Chatham is rather interesting. On 10 July 1814, three of James and Elizabeth's daughters, Mary Ann, Amelia and Caroline, were baptised in St Mary's church, Chatham. Nothing wrong in that, except that both Mary Ann and Amelia had already been baptised in St John's church, Portsea, Mary Ann in 1807 and Amelia in 1809. Clearly the parents wanted to make quite sure that the grace of God fell upon these two daughters.

In 1840 Elizabeth died aged 68. The cause of death was given as 'inflammation of the stomach'. Perhaps this was a loose term for appendicitis. James and Elizabeth were then living at Best Street, Chatham, a street which was to be connected with the family for generations to come. It would appear that after the death of his wife James went to live with Amelia, his only remaining unmarried daughter. The 1841 census for Chatham shows him as head of the household, living in Gage Lane, Chatham with Amelia, then aged 32, and what appears to be Amelia's illegitimate daughter, also called Amelia.

In 1841 James made his will, a requirement of those serving in the Royal Navy. In this document he left all his possessions to Amelia, and after his death it was Amelia who was the recipient of the balance of his pension.

James died on 17 July 1845 at Gage Lane, aged 79.[3] The cause of death was given simply as 'Old Age'.

*The signature of James Hansford from a naval document*

*Notes*

1   There is a question mark over the actual year. I have seen some transcriptions indicating a marriage year of 1769. The original documents on film are in a poor condition and difficult to read. I am inclined to believe that 1768 is correct.

2   A cox'n (coxswain) was a helmsman (steering a vessel) or crew member in charge of a boat. In James's case I am inclined to think that he was in charge of the smaller boat that would ferry the captain around.

3   Discrepancies concerning James's age occur several times on naval documents. If he was born in 1770, he would have been around age 75 when he died. It is possible that both James and his relatives only had a vague idea of his true age.

# Brief details of Royal Navy ships on which James Hansford (senior) served[1]

| | | |
|---|---|---|
| 1788 | *Sprightly* | cutter[2] 10 guns<br>built Dover 1778<br>captured by French 1801<br>scuttled |
| 1790 | *St George* | 2$^{nd}$ rate[3] 98 guns<br>built Portsmouth 1785<br>wrecked 1811 |
| 1790 | *Childers* | brig/sloop[4] 14 guns<br>built River Thames 1778<br>broken up 1811 |
| 1793 | *Leviathan* | 3$^{rd}$ rate  74 guns<br>built Chatham 1790<br>sold 1848 |
| 1795 | *Sans Pareil*[5] | 3$^{rd}$ rate  80 guns<br>captured from French 1794<br>broken up 1842 |
| 1800 | *Guachapin* | brig  14 guns<br>captured from Spanish early 1800s<br>wrecked, salvaged and sold West Indies 1811 |
| 1801 | *Abundance*[6] | storeship  24 guns<br>built Bucklers Hard 1799<br>sold 1823 |
| 1805 | *Bonne Citoyenne*[7] | 6$^{th}$ rate  20 guns<br>captured from French 1796<br>sold 1819 |

| 1806 | *Thames* | 5<sup>th</sup> rate 32 guns |

1806     *Thames*     5th rate 32 guns
built Chatham 1805
broken up 1816

1808     *Alarm*     5th rate 32 guns
built Harwich 1758
broken up 1812

1810     *Armide*     5th rate 38 guns
capturen from French 1806
broken up 1815

1811[8]     *Brakel (Braakel)*     4th rate 54 guns
captured from Dutch 1796
sold 1814

*Notes*

1   Information about the ships on which James served was obtained from a list maintained by the navy pay office as a record of service.

2   A cutter was a small, single-masted ship. Extremely fast and well-armed for its size, it was often used on coastal or anti-smuggling duties.

3   Royal Navy ships were rated 1-6 according to the number of guns they carried and the strength of fire power. The more guns a ship had, the higher the rating and the more of a fighting weapon it was.

4   Brigs and sloops were the smaller vessels used by the Royal Navy.

5   A literal translation is 'without equal'.

6   James was promoted to boatswain (and warrant officer status) in 1801, and *Abundance* was the first ship he served on in his new role.

7    A literal translation is 'good citizen'.

8    James appears to have moved to Chatham around 1811/1813 and from that point on appears to have been on the books of Chatham dockyard as regards pay. He would have served on more ships based at Chatham during the period 1811-16 when he was retired from the service through ill health. His superannuation was paid through Chatham dockyard.

# THE ANCESTRY OF JAMES HANSFORD (SENIOR) 1770-1845

A familiar situation in family history is the inability to positively identify early ancestors. However, as stated in the previous section, detailed research indicates that James Hansford senior was born in the village of Swyre in Dorset to William Hansford (born in 1742) and Frances Tibby (or Tidby).

The church register states that William came from the village of Askerswell, which lies just to the north of Swyre. Askerswell is an area well populated with Hansford families, and finding James's forebears was not without its difficulties. The most likely parents for William, James's father, seem to have been William Hansford (born in 1706) and Hannah Roll (born in about 1710), whose marriage took place in Askerswell on 22 August 1731.

It looks from the records available as if William and Hannah moved to Eggardon, near Askerswell, at some time during their marriage, because some of their children, including William, are listed as having been born there. None of these early records gives a clue as to how William earned a living. However, given the locality, it is highly probable that he obtained a living from the land, as either a farmer or a farm worker.

Hannah died in 1788, and William a year later. Both interments were listed as 'poor burials', indicating that the couple had probably fallen on hard times and were no longer able to support themselves financially.

There is an interesting diversion in the history of William and Hannah's children. One of their sons, Joseph, married Ann Everleigh at Whitchurch Canonicorum, Dorset on 7 September 1777 and went on to have a number of children, including Joseph (baptised 28 March 1788), who made his living as a saddler and harness-maker in Dorchester. Joseph married Amelia Baker on 17 September 1817, and their son Charles eventually became an alderman and a Justice of the Peace. In the Borough Gardens of Dorchester stands an ornate tower clock, which Charles Hansford donated to the town in 1905. At the dedication ceremony, which was attended by the mayor and town councillors, the clock was set in motion by Charles Hansford himself. The plaque on the clock reads: 'This clock & tower

# THE HANSFORD FAMILY FROM EARLY RECORDS

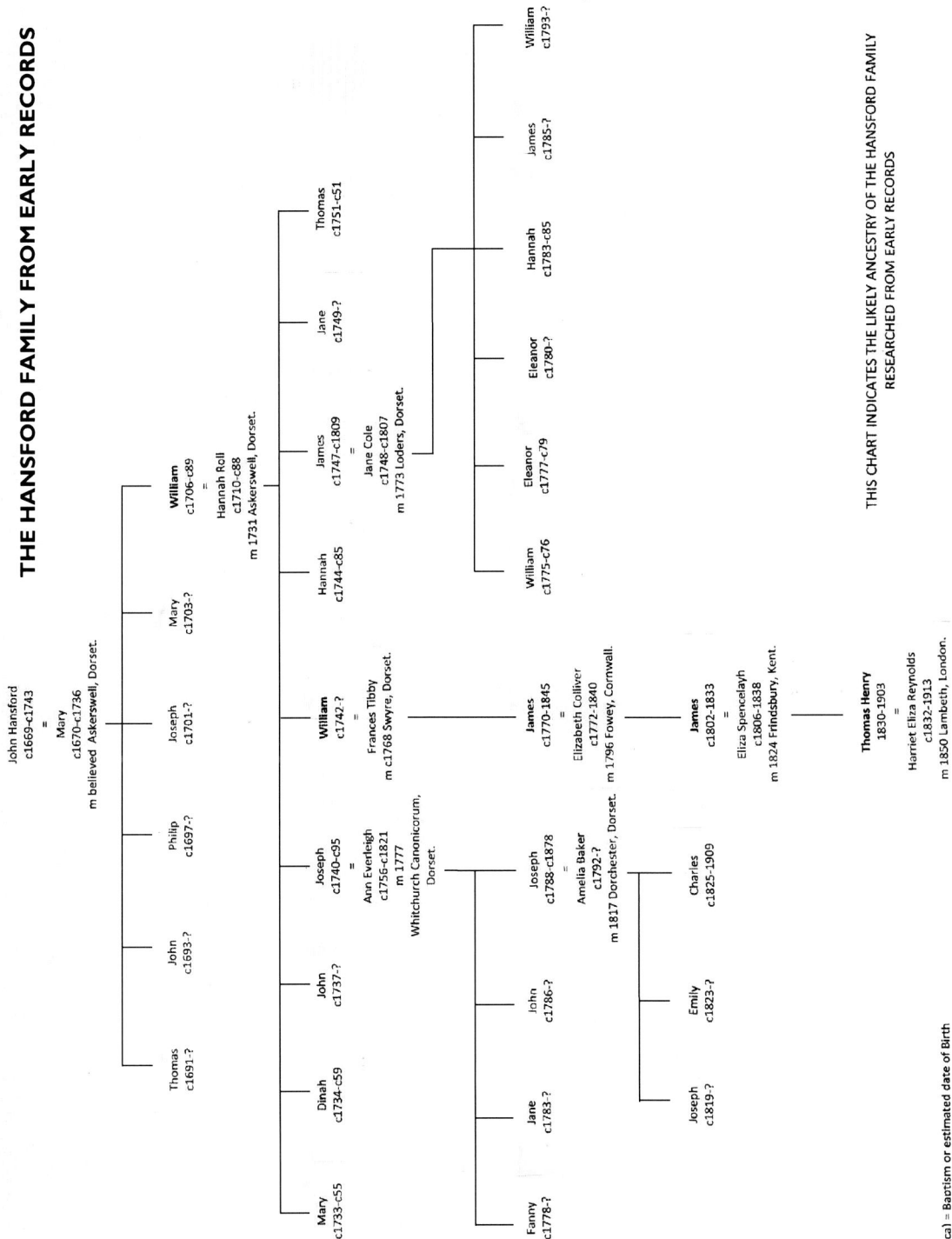

John Hansford
c1669-c1743
=
Mary
c1670-c1736
m believed Askerswell, Dorset.

Thomas
c1691-?

Dinah
c1734-c59

John
c1693-?

John
c1737-?

Philip
c1697-?

Joseph
c1740-c95
Ann Everleigh
c1756-c1821
m 1777
Whitchurch Canonicorum, Dorset.

Joseph
c1701-?

William
c1742-?
Frances Tibby
m c1768 Swyre, Dorset.

Mary
c1703-?

William
c1706-c89
=
Hannah Roll
c1710-c88
m 1731 Askerswell, Dorset.

Mary
c1733-c55

Jane
c1783-?

John
c1786-?

Joseph
c1788-c1878
Amelia Baker
c1792-?
m 1817 Dorchester, Dorset.

Fanny
c1778-?

Hannah
c1744-c85

James
c1770-1845
=
Elizabeth Colliver
c1772-1840
m 1796 Fowey, Cornwall.

William
c1775-c76

James
c1747-c1809
=
Jane Cole
c1748-c1807
m 1773 Loders, Dorset.

Jane
c1749-?

Thomas
c1751-c51

Eleanor
c1777-c79

Eleanor
c1780-?

Hannah
c1783-c85

James
c1785-?

William
c1793-?

Joseph
c1819-?

Emily
c1823-?

Charles
c1825-1909

James
c1802-1833
=
Eliza Spencelayh
c1806-1838
m 1824 Frindsbury, Kent.

Thomas Henry
1830-1903
=
Harriet Eliza Reynolds
c1832-1913
m 1850 Lambeth, London.

THIS CHART INDICATES THE LIKELY ANCESTRY OF THE HANSFORD FAMILY RESEARCHED FROM EARLY RECORDS

c (circa) = Baptism or estimated date of Birth

were presented to the Borough of Dorchester by Charles Hansford AD 1905'. In his will, dated 1906, Charles left the sum of £500 for the benefit of the museum and library in the town.

Seventeenth-century records tend to be vague and are sometimes in poor condition, but it is most likely that the parents of William Hansford, James senior's great-grandfather, were John Hansford, born about 1669, and Mary (surname unknown), born about 1670. They had at least four other children – Thomas (c1691), John (c1694), Joseph (c1701) and Mary (c1703).

I believe that the research for James senior's ancestry so far completed can be regarded as accurate. This produces a record going back to the 17th century, presenting a fascinating history of just one Hansford family over four centuries.

## Children of William Hansford and Hannah Roll

Mary (bapt. 10 June 1733)

Dinah (bapt. 3 February 1734/5)

John (bapt. 7 May 1737)

Joseph (bapt. 27 April 1740)

William (bapt. 12 December 1742)

Hannah (bapt. 25 November 1744)

James (bapt. 12 April 1747)

Jane (bapt. 20 August 1749)

Thomas (bapt. 27 October 1751)

## The following burials are listed:

John (17 April 1743)

Thomas (8 December 1751)

Mary (29 June 1755)

Dinah (29 May 1759)

# THE CHILDREN OF JAMES HANSFORD (SENIOR) AND ELIZABETH COLLIVER

### JOHN HANSFORD 1798-1829

Nine children are recorded as having been born to James and Elizabeth. The eldest of these was John, who was baptised in Fowey on 9 May 1798. John would have already been 13 or 14 years old when the family moved to Chatham from Portsea around 1812. It is quite possible that he had already started work by that time.

The next documented record of him after birth is his marriage on 5 July 1829 to Elizabeth Saxby, a widow, at St Margaret's church, Rochester. The marriage was of short duration: a burial is recorded for a John Hansford on 26 August 1829 at St Mary's parish church, Chatham. Though there is no definite proof that this is the John we are concerned with, it seems almost certain as no other burial appears in the records for a John Hansford at that time. In addition, the age and other details are correct.

Not only was Elizabeth a widow for the second time, but she was also pregnant. Her daughter Amelia Elizabeth was baptised on 28 April 1830. John's occupation is given as 'shoemaker'.

No further details have so far appeared about the life of Elizabeth. On 11 June 1853 Amelia Elizabeth married Charles Goff (or Gough – there is some confusion over the spelling) at St Mary's, Chatham. Charles Goff appears to have been a soldier at Chatham barracks.

### JAMES HANSFORD 1802-1833

Because James plays an important part in the family tree and is a direct link to the present generation, a separate section of this book is devoted to him.

# THE FAMILY OF AMELIA HANSFORD

**James Hansford**
**c1770-1845**
=
Elizabeth Colliver
c1772-1840

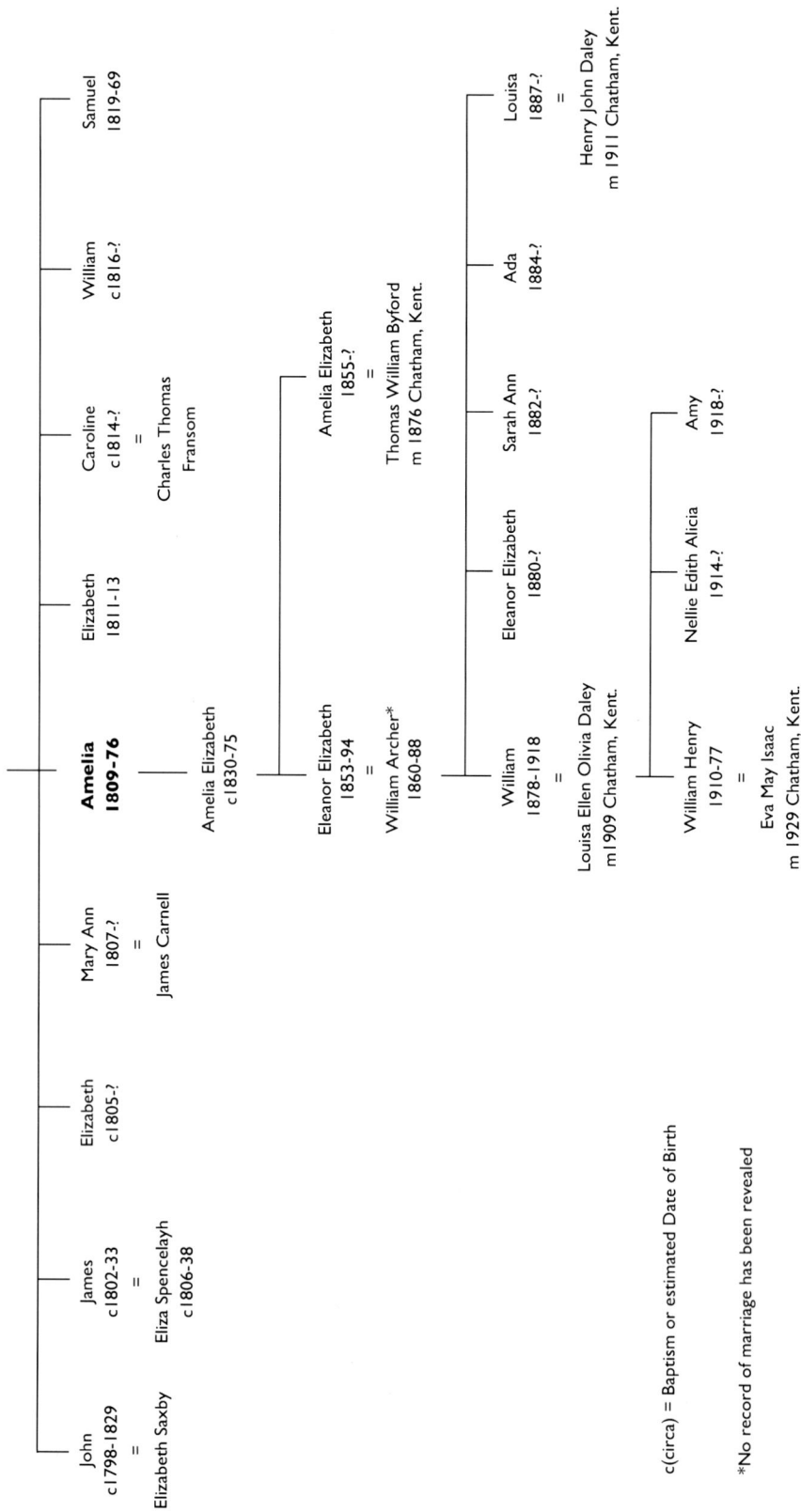

| | | | | | | | |
|---|---|---|---|---|---|---|---|
| John c1798-1829 | James c1802-33 | Elizabeth c1805-? | Mary Ann 1807-? | Amelia **1809-76** | Elizabeth 1811-13 | Caroline c1814-? | William c1816-? | Samuel 1819-69 |

John
c1798-1829
=
Elizabeth Saxby

James
c1802-33
=
Eliza Spencelayh
c1806-38

Mary Ann
1807-?
=
James Carnell

**Amelia**
**1809-76**

Caroline
c1814-?
=
Charles Thomas
Fransom

William
c1816-?

Samuel
1819-69

Amelia Elizabeth
c1830-75

Eleanor Elizabeth
1853-94
=
William Archer*
1860-88

Amelia Elizabeth
1855-?
=
Thomas William Byford
m 1876 Chatham, Kent.

William
1878-1918
=
Louisa Ellen Olivia Daley
m1909 Chatham, Kent.

Eleanor Elizabeth
1880-?

Sarah Ann
1882-?

Ada
1884-?

Louisa
1887-?
=
Henry John Daley
m 1911 Chatham, Kent.

William Henry
1910-77
=
Eva May Isaac
m 1929 Chatham, Kent.

Nellie Edith Alicia
1914-?

Amy
1918-?

c(circa) = Baptism or estimated Date of Birth

*No record of marriage has been revealed

### ELIZABETH HANSFORD 1805-?

Elizabeth appears to have been the third child of James and Elizabeth, and their first daughter. Records show that she was baptised in Fowey on 10 June 1805. Thereafter there is no trace of her. It seems that she died in childhood, because a second daughter named Elizabeth appears on the records for Portsea in 1811; but the fate of the first Elizabeth remains a mystery for the present.

### MARY ANN HANSFORD 1807-?

Mary Ann was one of the three children born in Portsea to James and Elizabeth. Her baptism was recorded in the parish church of St John's, Portsea on 19 March 1807, when she was 1 day old. Mary Ann would have been 5 or 6 years old when the family moved from Portsea to Chatham. The next time she appears on any records is in 1814 when she was baptised again, this time in the parish church of St Mary's, Chatham.

Mary married James Carnell on 31 October 1824 at All Saints parish church in Frindsbury, which is close to Chatham, only one month after her brother James was married in the same church.

### AMELIA HANSFORD 1809-1876

Of James and Elizabeth's five daughters, Amelia is the one we know the most about. We can piece together the story of her life because of the sad circumstances surrounding it.

Amelia was born on 6 August 1809 in Portsea. Her baptism took place on 27 August in St John's church, Portsea. She was baptised again on 10 July 1814 in St Mary's church, Chatham.

The next time we catch up with Amelia is in the 1841 census for Chatham, when she was living with her widowed father in Gage Lane. Although she was almost 32, her age was recorded as 30, in accordance with the requirement of the 1841 census that the ages of people over 15 be rounded down to the nearest five years. What is interesting is that she appears to have had an illegitimate daughter, called Amelia Elizabeth, then aged 12.

In 1845, when James Hansford died, he left all his possessions to his daughter Amelia.

On the 1851 census for Chatham, mother and daughter were living at Lower Whittaker Place, Chatham. Both gave their occupation as 'dressmaker'. However, the fact cannot be ignored that at that time prostitutes frequently described themselves as 'dressmakers' to avoid any embarrassment when talking to the census enumerator. It is quite possible that the two Amelias were indeed dressmakers. However, Chatham was a town teeming with sailors and soldiers, and the services of available women were much in demand. It would have been quite easy for both mother and daughter to earn a little bit on the side to make ends meet, perhaps when there was no work to be had in dressmaking. Certainly, as we shall see, with a few illegitimate children around, both women were not models of purity. In fairness, it has to be said that they were both consistent in maintaining that they were dressmakers on all the census forms on which they appear.

The 1861 census reveals a little more. Amelia, now 50, and her daughter, 31, were now living at 1 Kennards Cottages, Chatham. By this time Amelia's daughter, Amelia Elizabeth, also had two apparently illegitimate children: Eleanor Elizabeth, born on 31 July 1853, and Amelia Elizabeth, born on 21 December 1855. Also living with the family was Samuel, Amelia's younger brother, then aged 42 and receiving a pension from the Royal Navy. An interesting feature of Eleanor's birth certificate is that her father's name was recorded. This is not normally the case with illegitimate births at this period, either because the mother did not know who the father of the child was or the father refused to accept any responsibility. In Eleanor's case the father's name appears as William Burton, a lieutenant in the Royal Marines. One wonders whether he gave his consent, or whether Amelia Elizabeth just gave his name when asked. William Burton seems to have come from a very good family. Having a father from this background, though, certainly did not help poor Eleanor in later life.

Ten years on, the family fortunes were changing. Samuel, Amelia's brother, had died in 1869, and only Amelia's daughter Amelia Elizabeth and her two daughters appear on the 1871 census. Amelia Elizabeth's age is recorded as 38, but this cannot be correct: according to previous censuses she would have been nearer 42. Again her occupation appears as 'dressmaker', while that of her younger daughter, Amelia Elizabeth, was 'learning dressmaking', and Eleanor is listed as a servant. There is no mention of the original Amelia, James's daughter; nor has her name come to light anywhere else on the 1871 census. It could be that she is hidden with a wrongly spelt name or was simply passed over. It did happen.

In the 1870s tragedy started to overtake the family. On 28 June 1875 Amelia Elizabeth died. Her age appears on her death certificate as 40, and the cause of death as pulmonary phthisis – tuberculosis of the lungs. She died at Richard Street, Chatham, and the informant was her eldest daughter, Eleanor. It is interesting that Eleanor informed the registrar that her mother was the daughter of Richard Hansford, a warrant officer in the Royal Navy. This may or may not have been correct; to date I have not discovered any record of her birth.

Tracing Amelia after her daughter's death proved to be extremely difficult. For a long time it seemed that she had simply disappeared. Then one day I came across a death certificate for an Amelia Hainsford. There was no mention in any of the censuses of anyone of that name. Could it be an incorrect spelling? I went back to the records for St Mary's church, Chatham and sure enough that proved to be the case. This information gave new value to the death certificate. Poor Amelia died in Medway Union Workhouse in Chatham on 5 April 1876, aged 66, apparently from cirrhosis of the liver, a condition most likely brought on by excessive drinking.

Amelia's death certificate raises more questions than it answers. What really happened to her? How did she end up in the workhouse, and why did she turn to drink? Where were her two granddaughters? Was there an element of truth in the theory that she may have been a prostitute at times and that when she had lost her looks and her health broke down she was unable to find clients? Sadly, we shall probably never know the answer.

With the passing of Amelia in 1876 and her daughter Amelia Elizabeth in 1875 the family was reduced to the two granddaughters of the original Amelia: Eleanor Elizabeth* and Amelia Elizabeth.

## ELIZABETH HANSFORD 1811-1813

Elizabeth was born on 31 July 1811, while the family were living in Portsea, and was baptised in St John's church, Portsea. She had a very short life. She was buried at St Mary's church, Chatham on 11 February 1813, at the age of just 18 months. This tragedy must have occurred shortly after the family moved to Chatham from Portsea.

## CAROLINE HANSFORD 1814-?

Caroline was the only one of James and Elizabeth's daughters to have been born in Chatham. Records indicate that she was baptised there in the parish church of St Mary's on 10 of July 1814, together with her two older sisters Mary Ann and Amelia.

The only other information I have found about Caroline's early life is that her father James made an application for her to enter Greenwich Royal Hospital School in 1823.

---

* A detailed description of Eleanor Elizabeth's life appears in the first part of this book, in the section entitled *The Research Becomes More Intense.*

Though there are no records available confirming her entry and discharge, it is highly likely that she did attend this establishment.

The next document that comes to light concerning Caroline is a marriage certificate for the year 1839. On 23 January she married Charles Thomas Fransom, mariner, in the parish church of St Mary's, Chatham.

### WILLIAM HANSFORD 1816-?

William, the second-youngest son of James and Elizabeth, was born in Chatham on 7 January 1816. This information was confirmed when an application was made for him to enter Greenwich Royal Hospital School. Apparently it was discovered that William's baptism had been incorrectly entered under the name of Ansford. As a result his mother had to sign a statement to the effect that this was an error and state the exact birthdate.

William entered the school on 18 March 1825 and was discharged on 10 February 1830 to 'Chatham Flagship'. From this it can be deduced that he was intended for a naval career. This was not exceptional for boys who went to the school. The parents had to sign a document agreeing to the boy going into the naval service if required. As the school was supported by naval funds, it was not surprising that it was looked upon as a means of recruiting suitable boys for service in the navy or marines.

However, there is no record of young William having any contact with the navy after leaving the school. Perhaps he decided that life in the navy was not for him. What happened to him remains a mystery, as so far no trace of him has been discovered. A William Hansford is a witness at his sister Caroline's wedding in 1839. It is highly likely that this is the missing William, because as far as records show there was no other William in the family at that period.

### SAMUEL COLLIVER HANSFORD 1819-1869

Samuel Colliver, the youngest son of James and Elizabeth, was baptised in Chatham on 2 May 1819 in the parish church of St Mary's, taking as his second name his mother's maiden name.

By 1819 his father had retired on a pension from the navy, but he applied for Samuel to enter Greenwich Royal Hospital School. The vital acceptance letter from the school is missing from the records, but in view of Samuel's subsequent career it is highly likely that he was educated there. It would have been logical for the application from such a long-serving officer as James to be regarded favourably.

Samuel entered the service of the Royal Navy on the 27 October 1832 on board HMS *Forester* and had a long and full career. He retired in 1861, having exceeded the naval service of his father by two years.

On the 1861 census, Samuel was recorded as living with his sister Amelia at Kennard's Cottages, Chatham.

He died of dysentery in hospital on 16 November 1869, aged 50.

## Royal Navy ships on which Samuel Colliver Hansford served, with brief details of each ship's history

| 1832 | *Forester* | brig-sloop | 10 guns<br>built Chatham 1832<br>sold 1843 |
| 1833 | *Thunderer* | 2nd rate | 84 guns<br>built Woolwich 1831<br>sold 1901 |
| 1837 | *Castor* | 5th rate | 26 guns<br>built Chatham 1832<br>sold 1902 |
| 1841 | *Thunderer* | 2nd rate | details above |
| 1843 | *Anson* | 3rd rate | 74 guns<br>built near Hull 1812<br>convict ship Tasmania 1844<br>broken up Hobart 1851 |
| 1843 | *Penelope* | 5th rate | 46 guns<br>built Chatham 1829<br>sold 1864 (for breaking up) |

| 1843 | *Poictiers* | 3rd rate | 74 guns<br>built by King, Upnor (near Chatham) 1809<br>broken up Chatham 1857 |
| 1844 | *Collingwood* | 3rd rate | 80 guns<br>built Pembroke 1841<br>sold 1867 |
| 1852 | *Modeste* | sloop | 18 guns<br>built Woolwich 1837<br>sold 1866 |
| 1853 | *Sphynx* | wood paddle sloop | built Woolwich 1846<br><br>broken up Devonport 1881 |
| 1854 | Employed at Chatham dockyard[1] | | |
| 1854 | *Arab* | brig-sloop | 16 guns<br>built Chatham 1847<br>broken up Chatham 1879 |
| 1857 | *Waterloo* | 1st rate | 120 guns<br>built Chatham 1833<br>accidentally burnt river Thames 1918 |
| 1857 | Employed at Chatham dockyard | | |
| 1857 | *Heron* | brig | 16 guns<br>built Chatham 1847<br>foundered 1859 |
| 1859 | *Victory* | 1st rate | 100 guns<br>built Chatham 1765 |

|      |                |                       |                             |
|------|----------------|-----------------------|-----------------------------|
|      |                |                       | rebuilt 1801                |
|      |                |                       | harbour service 1824        |
|      |                |                       | dry docked Portsmouth 1922  |
| 1859 | *Wellesley*    | 3rd rate              | 74 guns                     |
|      |                |                       | built Bombay 1815           |
|      |                |                       | sunk in an air raid 1940    |
| 1860 | *Miranda*      | wood screw corvette   | 14 guns                     |
|      |                |                       | built Sheerness 1851        |
|      |                |                       | sold 1869                   |
| 1860 | *Royal Adelaide* | 1st rate            | 104 guns                    |
|      |                |                       | built Plymouth 1827         |
|      |                |                       | depot ship 1860             |
|      |                |                       | sold 1905                   |
| 1861 | *Fisgard*      | 5th rate              | 46 guns                     |
|      |                |                       | built Pembroke 1819         |
|      |                |                       | depot ship 1848             |
|      |                |                       | broken up 1879              |

*Note*

1    During the period of time that Samuel served in the navy, continuous service arrangements did not exist.

He would have been free to take up work in the dockyard in preference to life at sea if he so desired.

# JAMES HANSFORD (JUNIOR) 1802-1833

For the purpose of this research James is the most important of James Hansford and Elizabeth Colliver's children because he is a direct ancestor of mine. Fortunately, he pursued a naval career, and it is from these records that most of the details of his life have been revealed.

James was born in Fowey while the family was still living there. He was baptised on 29 December 1802 in the parish church of St Fimbarrus. One naval record states his place of birth to be Hill Street, Fowey, a street that does not appear to exist under that name today, though there are several older streets in Fowey that climb steeply out of the small town and could qualify.

In 1813 his father, who was still serving as a boatswain in the navy at Chatham, made an application for young James to go to Greenwich Royal Hospital School. From the brief documents that still exist, it looks as if he was admitted to the school, though any further information seems to have been lost. His next appearance in the records is as a boy serving on HMS *Blossom*, which more or less confirms his stay at the school, because a high percentage of the pupils ended up on naval ships after their four years there.

James's next available record shows him serving on a ship called the *Prince Regent*. The year was 1823 and James was listed as an able seaman, indicating that by this time he was an experienced seaman with a few years at sea.

James served on the *Prince Regent* from 1823 to 1831, quite a long period for a seaman to stay with one ship. He then served for a few months on the *Royal George*, before signing on board HMS *Ocean* later in 1831. He remained with the *Ocean* until he was discharged on 14 August 1833. The reason for this discharge remains a mystery. *Ocean* was based at Chatham, so that would clearly have been an attraction for a local man.

The record of James's marriage was extremely difficult to find. Various church records were consulted without success, including those in Chatham and Portsmouth, but no hint of where the marriage took place came to light. Oddly, as is often the case, it was while I was occupied with researching something else that a clue appeared. While I was looking at the application papers for James's son Thomas Henry to enter Greenwich Royal Hospital School, I realised that not all the documents were present. To support an application to enter the school, an official record of the father's naval service had to be obtained from the navy pay office, and this document, together with the applicant's parents' marriage certificate, had to accompany the application. In Thomas Henry's case the marriage certificate was missing, but a note had been made on the application papers that this document had been seen and then returned to Thomas Henry. What was interesting was that the brief note referred to a marriage for Thomas Henry's parents in Frindsbury, which is just across the Medway from Chatham.

This called for another visit to the record office in Strood, which is close to Chatham. I chose a Saturday morning for this trip, and an hour's work with the marriage records for All Saints church, Frindsbury provided the information I was seeking. Though the records were in a pretty bad state and not easy to read, it was possible to confirm that James Hansford, a bachelor, married Eliza Spencelayh*, a spinster, on 26 September 1824. One of the witnesses was Elizabeth Hansford, possibly James's mother. Three children are recorded for the marriage: John James Colliver in 1828, my great-grandfather Thomas Henry in 1830, and Eliza Ann in 1832.

Within a few days of being paid off from HMS *Ocean*, James contracted cholera and died. His funeral took place in Chatham parish church on 24 August 1833. He was 30 years old. There were several outbreaks of cholera in England during the 19th century, and

* Only a small amount of information has so far been gleaned about the Spencelayh family (sometimes spelt Spenceley). The parish records of St Margaret of Antioch, Rochester indicate that Eliza, daughter of Thomas and Mary Spencelayh, was born on 24 January 1806 and baptised on 21 of February in the same year.

There is strong evidence that Eliza had more than one sister. A Mary Spenceley married William Moses Trice on 8 April 1828 in Rochester, and an Ann Spenceley married a Thomas Jasper in St Nicholas Church, Deptford on 12 June 1834. Deptford, which is close to Greenwich, had been an important naval dockyard since the 15th century. This and other pieces of evidence appear to indicate that the Spencelayh family also had strong connections to the sea, many of the men being mariners. Another possible member of the family features in 1841 when Thomas Henry, the youngest son of James and Eliza Hansford, was admitted to Greenwich Hospital School. The consent form was signed by an Elizabeth Spenceley. It is possible that Elizabeth was Eliza's sister or sister-in-law.

Though the name Spencelayh (or Spenceley) does not appear to have its roots in the county of Kent, quite a number of people bearing it appear in the records of Medway and the surrounding area. Again, this could be due to links with the sea and the moving about of sailors. So far one other record has been discovered that could be related to my family. A Mary Spenceley, aged 67, was buried in St Mary's church, Chatham on 17 December 1834. It is possible that she was Eliza's mother, but I have not been able to establish this.

Chatham did not escape. A major one started in 1832 and it looks as if either James caught the tail end of this one or it was a further minor outbreak, as he and a number of other local people died from it in 1833. Cholera frequently proved to be rapidly fatal, with victims often dying in anything from 3 to 18 hours after the first symptoms appeared.

Eliza was left with three young children to support. More information about this is in the separate section dealing with Thomas Henry.

*Gun Wharf and St Mary's church Chatham*

# THE CHILDREN OF JAMES HANSFORD (JUNIOR) AND ELIZA SPENCELAYH

### JOHN JAMES COLLIVER HANSFORD 1828-?

John James Colliver was the eldest son of James Hansford and Eliza Spencelayh. Very little about him appears to be documented, but we know that he was born in Chatham in 1828 and that Colliver was his grandmother's maiden name. Only one reference to him after that has been discovered. This is in a letter written by an aunt at the time of his brother Thomas Henry's entry to Greenwich Royal Hospital School. By that time John James Colliver and his brother and sister were orphans and were apparently being looked after by an aunt. In the letter this aunt mentions 'looking after another twelve year old boy'. This would almost certainly have been a reference to John James Colliver.

After that there is no further trace of him. At the time, close on 200 years ago, although official records were in place, they were not strictly adhered to, and there was no enforcement by law until the 1870s. People could slip through the net, and a birth or a death could go unrecorded. It is almost certain that many ships carried crew members who were not on the books. For the family historian situations like this create problems, producing loose ends that are difficult to tie up or gaps in the family tree that take a long time to fill in. My belief is that John James Colliver most likely went to sea and disappeared there, as despite arduous searching I have not managed to find any trace of him on later census returns or in other official records. He may also have contributed to the family legend of brothers being lost at sea and years later reinforced his brother Thomas Henry's decision to move away from the sea. Given the length of time that has elapsed, it is quite possible the truth about his fate may never be discovered.

**THOMAS HENRY HANSFORD 1830-1903**

Because Thomas Henry was a direct ancestor of mine, a detailed description of his life is given under a separate heading.

**ELIZA ANN HANSFORD 1832-?**

The baptism for Eliza Ann was recorded in the register of the parish church of St Mary's, Chatham on 22 July 1832. Sadly, she was only 1 year old when her father died of cholera. Thereafter her young life must have been very hard. Her mother remarried in 1835, but tragically died 3 years later, leaving 6-year-old Eliza Ann an orphan, together with her two brothers, John James Colliver and Thomas Henry. There was also a baby from the second marriage, who lived only a few months.

With her nearest brother in age sent away to school in Greenwich and her eldest brother making his own way, little Eliza Ann must have had a lonely life. She was probably brought up by other members of the family and sent into service when she was old enough. On the 1841 census she appears with her brother Thomas Henry living with an Ann Jasper, who was the wife of another seaman and was listed as being of 'independent means'. There is evidence that Ann was a relative, most likely an aunt. The next time Eliza Ann appeared in records was in 1850, when on 22 January it appears that she gave birth to an illegitimate son, whom she named John James. On 22 August 1852 she married William Witmore, a 28-year-old mariner, in Chatham, though both bride and groom list their place of residence as Chatham's neighbour Rochester. So far research has not revealed any more information about the subsequent life of either Eliza Ann or her son John James.

# THOMAS HENRY HANSFORD 1830-1903

Thomas Henry Hansford was born on 7 March 1830 and baptised three weeks later in St Mary's church, Chatham.

Sadly, he was to lose his father almost without knowing him. In the month of August 1833, James Hansford left his ship HMS *Ocean* in Chatham and within days succumbed to cholera.

James's widow, Eliza, was left with three small children to support: John, aged 5, Thomas Henry, aged 3, and Eliza, only 1 year old. One can only imagine the trauma of losing a husband and provider at a time before the welfare state, when the only refuge for the destitute, unless there were other family members to help out, was the parish workhouse.

Eliza may have been fortunate in having family members to help her. There is some evidence for this. Her husband's brothers and sisters lived in Chatham, as did her husband's parents, though by this time they would have been aged and possibly infirm. Eliza herself appears to have been a local woman, perhaps with brothers and sisters living in the area. It would probably have been the women in the family who gave a woman in Eliza's situation the most support.

At that time a widow with dependent children would remarry as soon as a reasonable time had elapsed since her husband's death. Many women had no means of earning a living unless they were single and childless and could go into service; those with children were obliged to find a husband and provider as soon as possible. Eliza followed this pattern: she married another seaman, Henry Gage, on 28 June 1835. Sadly the marriage was brief: Eliza died in December 1838 at the age of 32, leaving a 3-month-old son as well as her other three children.

However, before her death she had applied to have Thomas Henry admitted to Greenwich Royal Hospital School. This school was part of the Royal Hospital for Seamen, which had been a project of Queen Mary II and dates back to 1694. The Royal Hospital School started some years later for the sons and daughters of men who had served in the

Royal Navy. Normally the applicants had to be orphans or the family had to be in some distress or need. Applicants had to be between the ages of 9 and 11, without any infirmity and be able to read and write simple text. On discharge at the age of 14 the boys were usually sent to sea on a navy ship and the girls were sent into service. While at the school a uniform was worn and the discipline was strict. At the time of Thomas Henry's placement the school had places for 400 boys and 200 girls. It is quite feasible that the idea to send Thomas Henry there originated from his grandfather James, long retired and living close by in Chatham. James appeared to have had a high regard for the school, having made application for at least four of his own children to go there.

Initially the application for Thomas Henry did not appear to be successful; queries regarding his father's naval service caused a delay. The application was pursued in 1840, after Eliza's death, by Mary Trice, who describes herself as Thomas Henry's aunt. She also indicated that she had been looking after all three children. She was probably Eliza's sister: a Mary Spenceley married William Moses Trice in the church of St Margaret, Rochester on

*A Boy from Greenwich Royal Hospital School*

H. M. Ship Brune,
Chatham, 31st May, 1838.-

Sir,

I take the liberty of forwarding to you Testimonials of my late husband (James Hansford a seaman,) who has served in the Navy, and who died in August, 1833, leaving a family of three children; and as one of them (a boy) who attained the age of 9 years, in march last, I feel desirous of getting him into the Lower School at Greenwich, hoping, Sir, you will be pleased to take the case into your consideration and render me aid in this particular, as it will be doing me a great service.

I am,

Sir,

Your most obedient and obliged Servant,

Eliza Gage

P.S. He has also served in the Ocean and as near as I can recollect, (the certificate being lost) it was from 1831 to 1833.-

To, P. L. Le Geyt, Esquire
Clerk of the Check,
Royal Hospital,
Greenwich

*The first application letter dated May 1838*

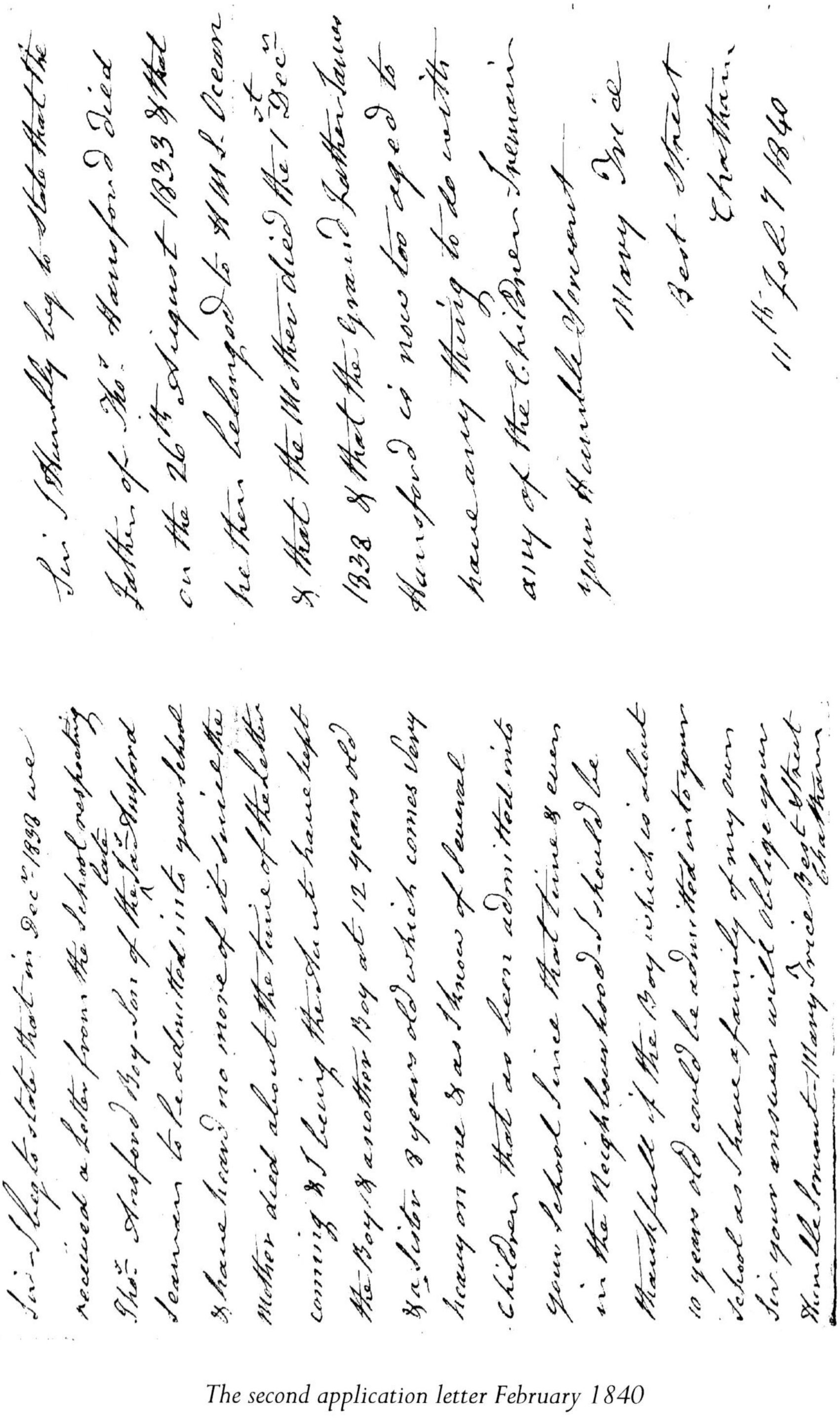

Sir - I beg to state that in Decr 1838 we
received a Letter from the School respecting
Thos Ansford Boy - Son of the late Jas Ansford
Seaman to be admitted into your School
& have heard no more of it since the
Mother died about the time of the Letter
coming & I being the Aunt have kept
the Boy & another Boy at 12 years old
& a Sister 8 years old which comes very
heavy on me & as I know of Several
Children that as been admitted into
your School Since that time & even
in the Neighbourhood - I should be
thankfull if the Boy which is about
10 years old could be admitted into your
School as I have a family of my own
Sir your answer will Oblige your
Humble Servant - Mary Trice Best Street
Chatham

Sir I Humbly beg to State that the
Father of Thos Hansford died
on the 26th August 1833 & that
he then belonged to H M S Ocean
& that the Mother died the 1st Decr
1838 & that the Grand Father James
Hansford is now too aged to
have any thing to do with
any of the Children - I remain
your Humble Servant
Mary Trice
Best Street
Chatham
11th Feby 1840

*The second application letter February 1840*

*Duplicate*

Royal Hospital, Greenwich,
14 Aug.t 1841.

Eliz.t Spencley

The Governor having approved of the selection of Thos H. Hansford (4033) to be admitted into the Lower School of this Institution, upon condition that you sign the engagement on the other side hereof; you are desired to cause him to attend at the Office of the Clerk of the Cheque, on the 14th Sept.r

between the hours of nine and eleven o'Clock, bringing this Letter, signed as above directed.

I am,

Your obedient Servant,

*for* Clerk of the Cheque.

NOTE.—It is expected that the Child will be brought in a clean, wholesome state; his hair closely cut, and his head free from Nits, &c. but that it will be perfectly useless to bring him if he has any impediment of speech, any infirmity of body or mind, or if he has any Ring-worm, or soreness of head, or is afflicted with any temporary disease whatever.

*The final acceptance letter dated August 1841*

I *Elizabeth Spencerley*, do hereby agree that *Thos. H. Housford*, if admitted into the Lower School of the Royal Hospital at Greenwich, shall remain there as long as may be deemed proper; and that he shall be at the disposal of the Authorities thereof, to serve in the Royal Navy, Royal Marines, or the Merchant Service, if considered expedient.

*The mark of*
Elizabeth X Spencerley

*Witness*

*The agreement letter September 1841*

*Thomas Henry Hansford 1830-1903 and Harriet Eliza Hansford (Reynolds)*

8 April 1828. Mary Trice was also the informant on Eliza's death certificate and that of the 5-month-old child from Eliza's second marriage.

At the time of the 1841 census, Thomas Henry and his sister Eliza were living with Ann Jasper and her young family. There is no mention of the two children's older brother John. Mary Trice had indicated in a letter to Greenwich Royal Hospital School when making application for Thomas Henry to go there that she found the task of looking after three children in addition to her own a difficult task, so perhaps Ann Jasper had taken on their care.

Thomas Henry entered the school on 4 September 1841 and remained there until 14 May 1845. When he left, the records show that he was discharged 'to friends'. There is no indication of who these friends were. Although one of the prime objects of Greenwich Royal Hospital School was to groom boys for service in the Royal Navy or the Royal Marines, they did not always go on to such a career. In peacetime, the navy had plenty of hands and was not in immediate need of seamen, unlike in times of war, when ships were urgently being made ready for sea and action.

It is unprofessional in family history research to assume anything without the necessary evidence. However, in the case of Thomas Henry and the 'friends' into whose care he was

*St John the Evangelist, Waterloo, London*

delivered, there are little shreds of possible evidence, and these may lie with the woman who became his wife five years later, Harriet Eliza Reynolds. The couple were married on 17 November 1850 in the parish church of St John the Evangelist, Waterloo Road, London. The witnesses shown on the marriage certificate were Thomas and Elizabeth Reynolds, who must have been the bride's parents. Why Thomas Henry and Harriet Eliza married in Waterloo is another mystery; perhaps Harriet Eliza was in service there. It is possible that Thomas Henry's work also took him there. He was a journeyman whitesmith by trade, which means that he did not have a permanent place of employment but moved around as work availability dictated. There is one other clue from Thomas Henry's early life. Thomas Reynolds, his father-in-law, was a Greenwich pensioner, which means he was receiving a pension after a career in the Royal Navy. It is just possible that Thomas Henry met his future father-in-law during his four years at the naval school. He might even have lodged with him.

On the 1851 census, a few months after their marriage, Thomas Henry and Harriet Eliza are shown to be living in Greenwich. It is interesting that Harriet Eliza's parents occupied the house next door.

The young couple's first child was born on 9 September 1852 and baptised in St Alfege church, Greenwich. The baby was named Thomas Henry. Their address was given as Lower Park Street, Greenwich.

During the early part of their married life, Thomas Henry and Harriet Eliza moved around a good deal: Greenwich, Chatham, back to Greenwich, Chatham again, Loose (near Maidstone), and back to London. All their children were born at different addresses, over a period of ten years or so. This was no doubt dictated by the nature of Thomas Henry's job: he had a family to support and had to go where the work was. Our working-class Victorian ancestors moved house a lot more than we might think. Surprisingly, this was not so difficult in those days. The tiny houses they occupied were rented for an affordable sum on a weekly basis, and all that was required when they needed to move was to collect together the family's possessions – often not much more than a few pieces of basic furniture and cooking utensils – and load these onto a handcart. If their new accommodation was not within easy walking distance, a carrier with a horse and cart was usually available for a reasonable sum. For longer journeys, the railways were now well established. Thomas Henry would have been able to travel from Greenwich to Chatham by train.

Harriet Eliza gave birth to eleven children who are documented on records:
Thomas Henry 1852
Elizabeth Ann 1855
Mary Ann 1857
William Charles 1858
Caroline Elizabeth 1860
Charles Saunders 1862
John James 1864
Elizabeth Reynolds 1866
Frederick Edwin 1869
Fanny Ada Charlotte 1870
Harriet Georgina 1872

Sadly, Elizabeth Ann died in 1858 and Caroline Elizabeth in 1879. The other children survived into adulthood and all except one son eventually married.

In the 1870s, their lives changed radically when Thomas Henry moved his entire family, with the exception of his eldest son, north to the industrial town of Wigan. One can only imagine the effect this must have had on them. This would have been an entirely new way of life in a completely different environment. Exactly when they moved is difficult to establish, but some indication can be obtained from two dated bits of evidence. The first is a photograph taken in London in 1874 that shows Thomas Henry and Harriet Eliza's son William Charles at the age of 15; the second is the record of the death of their daughter Caroline Elizabeth in Wigan in 1879. The move would almost certainly have taken place between those two dates.

Why did the family make the long journey to a new life in Wigan? Family legend, as I have already related, tells that the move was prompted by the loss of one of Thomas Henry's close relatives at sea. Perhaps there is an element of truth in the tale, but there may well have been an economic reason for this dramatic change in their lives. The cotton industry was booming in Lancashire. Workers were badly needed, and a skilled engineer such as Thomas Henry would have been welcome. With a family to feed, did he come to the conclusion that the expanding North offered them all more opportunities? We shall probably never know the real reason for the move.

Once in Wigan, the family settled at 4 Miry Lane, where they remained for thirty years or so. In those days Miry Lane was a fairly short street of small houses. One end of the street supported a railway bridge with a narrow arch, and the other led to the main road to the centre of the town. At this end stood Thomas Taylor's Victoria Mills. It is possible that Thomas Henry found employment there. He would not have had very far to walk to work: number 4 was no more than three minutes' walk away. Today, there are no houses in Miry Lane. They were all pulled down in recent years and a collection of small industrial units occupy the area now. Victoria Mills has become the offices for Shearings the coach operator and holiday company.

Thomas Henry died on 9 June 1903, aged 73, at 4 Miry Lane. The cause of death was given as cardiac disease and dropsy. He is buried in Wigan Borough cemetery, Lower Ince, Wigan.

# THE CHILDREN OF THOMAS HENRY HANSFORD
# AND HARRIET ELIZA REYNOLDS

### THOMAS HENRY HANSFORD 1852-1931

Thomas Henry was the eldest son of Thomas Henry and Harriet Eliza. He was born on 9 September 1852 and baptised in St Alfege church, Greenwich on 2 October the same year. The last documented record of him is on the 1861 census. Ten years later, the family was living at Loose near Maidstone, but he was not present on the night of the census. In that interval he completely disappeared from the records.

What happened to him? In the early days of my research it was impossible to tell. My father once remarked, 'We think he went to Australia', meaning that this was the belief that existed in the family a generation later. I always felt that there must be some truth in the story, and it seemed logical to pursue this theory in attempting to solve the mystery of young Thomas Henry's disappearance.

From information received directly from Australia, there is now sufficient evidence to indicate that he did indeed eventually settle in Australia and raise a family there. More information on the research involved and details discovered is recorded in detail in the section of this book entitled The Australian Link.

### ELIZABETH ANN HANSFORD 1855-1858

Elizabeth Ann was born on 2 December 1855 at 48 Lower Park Street, Greenwich, and her birth was registered on 7 January 1856. The informant was her father, and it is interesting that he gave his occupation as 'blacksmith (journeyman)'.

Sadly, Elizabeth Ann died on 28 September 1858. The cause of death was given as 'fever for 4 days and convulsions for one day'. The informant was H.E. Hansford, 'present at death'. The family was living at Best Street, Chatham.

**MARY ANN HANSFORD 1857-?**

Mary Ann was born on 27 April 1857, while the family was still living at 48 Lower Park Street, Greenwich. Thomas Henry registered the birth of his new daughter on 6 June 1857.

Mary Ann was the first of the daughters to leave home; she married John Jones, a railway pointsman, on 3 February 1883 at St Thomas's church, Wigan. It is interesting that on the marriage certificate her name appears as Mary Ann Eliza Hansford. The name Eliza is not on her birth certificate.

John and Mary Ann later settled in Southport. On the 1911 census they were recorded as living in Virginia Street, Southport. John had changed his occupation and was now a railway signalman. Also at the address were their three daughters, Harriet Hansford, aged 26, Elizabeth Ada, aged 25, and Lilian, aged 21, and their son Frederick, aged 17. Elizabeth Ada and Lilian are listed as dressmakers, and Harriet as a shop assistant. Frederick appears to have followed his father to become a railway employee: he is listed as a railway clerk.

An interesting feature of this census return is that Harriet Eliza, Mary Ann's widowed mother, was also in the household. Though she was listed as a dependant, there is no way of telling whether her stay was intended to be temporary or more permanent. She later moved back to Wigan, where her death was recorded in 1913.

I have so far been unable to find any record of Mary Ann's death.

**WILLIAM CHARLES HANSFORD 1858-1926**

Thomas Henry and his family were living in Best Street, Chatham when William Charles, their second son and my grandfather, was born on 3 December 1858. Thomas Henry and Harriet Eliza would still have been grieving for the loss of their little daughter Elizabeth Ann a few months previously, so a new baby might have brought them comfort. This time the parents took several months to register the birth. Harriet Eliza performed this task on 10 March 1859. On this certificate Thomas Henry's occupation appears as 'whitesmith'.

Detailed information about William Charles and his family appears in a separate section.

**CAROLINE ELIZABETH HANSFORD 1860-1879**

When Caroline Elizabeth was born on 22 August 1860, Thomas Henry, Harriet Eliza and their children were still living in Chatham, though their address was now Cooks Wharf. Thomas Henry registered the birth on 1 October 1860. It is interesting that on this occasion he again recorded his occupation as a blacksmith. It is quite possible that, being trained in metal working, he was able to adapt his skills as required to keep in work and maintain his increasing family. By the time Caroline Elizabeth was born, her mother already had an 8-year-old son, a 2-year-old daughter and another baby of just 20 months.

Caroline Elizabeth would have been a teenager when the family moved to Wigan. It is not certain that she would have been able to work. On 23 June 1879, she died at the family home, 4 Miry Lane, Wigan. The cause of death was given as morbus cordis, a medical term for heart disease. According to the death certificate she had had this condition for twelve months. A secondary cause was ascites (fluid retention), from which she had suffered for the last fourteen days of her life. Given the serious nature of her complaint, it is quite possible that she was already in poor health when the family made the move to Wigan. It is sad to think that her ill health probably prevented her from taking an active part in the family's new life in the north of England.

The informant on the death certificate was Mary Ann, Caroline Elizabeth's 22-year-old sister, who was present at the time of death.

### CHARLES SAUNDERS HANSFORD 1862-1940

When Charles Saunders was born on 13 August 1862, Thomas Henry had moved his family back to Greenwich, where they were recorded as living at 12 Clarks Buildings. The registration of the new baby was carried out by his mother on 22 September 1862. Once again the father's occupation was given as 'whitesmith'.

The baby's second name is intriguing. It was not uncommon for our Victorian ancestors to give their children a second name taken from grandparents. In Charles Saunders's case, however, research has so far not revealed the source of this name.

Charles Saunders appears to have at first followed the local tradition of working in the cotton industry, but later he became a hairdresser, his occupation when he married Eliza Storey on 1 January 1887 at the Methodist church in Bolton.

The couple's first child, Violet, was born on 29 October that same year, when they were living at 11 Palmerston Road, Little Bolton.

Just over twelve months later, on 21 November 1888, their only son, Harry, was born at 80 Blackburn Road, Little Bolton. 18 May 1890 saw the birth of another daughter, Harriet

Eliza, at the same address. After a gap of five years, their fourth and final child, Henrietta Frances May, appeared on 15 March 1895. Eliza, who registered the birth, recorded her husband's occupation as 'master hairdresser'.

Little is known about the family from then on, apart from the information in official documents. The first date of any note was the marriage of Harriet at the age of 23 to 25-year-old Wilfred Mayoh, a cotton worker, on 11 April 1914 at Raikes Parade Methodist church, Blackpool.

It is intriguing that at the time of her marriage Harriet gave her address as 34 Bank Road Blackpool, while that of the groom was 1504, Rumworth Road, Lostock. Lostock is near Bolton. Perhaps it may be deduced from this situation that Harriet was working in Blackpool when she met her husband-to-be. The couple took up residence in Blackpool, and appeared to remain there.

On the marriage certificate the bride's brother and sister, Harry and Hettie (Henrietta), are shown as witnesses.

Harry remained single until 1920. On 21 February, in the parish church of St Saviour, Manchester, he married Emily Mary Hore from the parish of New Brighton, a small town on the river Mersey close to Liverpool. He gave his occupation as 'electrician'. Once again, Hettie was one of the witnesses.

Harry died of pulmonary tuberculosis on 27 June 1948, aged 59. His place of death was given as Birkenhead, and his occupation as 'electrician – ship repairs'.

Sadness came to Charles Saunders and Eliza again in 1923. On 16 August, at the family home at 12 Marlborough Street, Bolton, their 28-year-old unmarried daughter, Henrietta, died of pulmonary phthisis (tuberculosis of the lungs). Apparently Henrietta had earnt her living as a shorthand typist; this was quite an achievement at that time, as most women of her generation would have been cotton operatives in the mills.

The eldest daughter of the family, Violet, a sewing machinist, remained unmarried and lived to the age of 75. She died from heart failure on 18 February 1963 at 9 Henry Street, Bolton. The informant for the death certificate was her brother-in-law, Wilfred Mayoh.

Eliza died on 18 November 1928 in Townleys Hospital, Farnworth, near Bolton. She was 64. Charles Saunders, who registered her death, gave his address as 19 Victoria Grove, Bolton.

The 1930s brought the Great Depression and the hunger marches of the north of England, although as a hairdresser Charles Saunders perhaps survived better than many.

Charles Saunders died on 5 December 1940. In the last months of life he would have seen the gradual slide into war for the second time in his lifetime. Once again, the informant on the death certificate was his son-in-law Wilfred Mayoh. The address was given as 9 Henry

Street, Bolton, the same address where his daughter Violet was living at the time of her death twenty-three years later.

## JAMES JOHN HANSFORD 1864-1923

James John is the member of Thomas Henry's family about whom we know the least. He was born on 12 October 1864 at 36 Trafalgar Grove, Greenwich. The family had been living in Greenwich for about four years and now included Thomas Henry (junior), aged 12, Mary Ann, aged 7, William Charles, aged 5, Caroline Elizabeth, aged 4, and Charles Saunders, aged 2.

James John appears on the 1871 census, when the family was still living in London, but the 1881 census, which for the first time shows Thomas Henry and his family living in Wigan, reveals more information about him. On this document James John is listed as an 'imbecile'. Not too much should be read into this statement. The wording enumerators of the day were instructed to use in their descriptions was extremely limited.

It is quite possible that James John was brain-damaged. What is clear is that whatever the problem was, it prevented him from living what might be termed a normal life.

On the 1891 census, he is once again described as an imbecile. After that date he completely disappears from records. There is no mention of him in Wigan on the 1901 census.

Finding James John after 1891 proved to be difficult. It was several years before I managed to find out what happened to him. The 1901 census was not yet available. I searched the death records in vain. It was while I was looking for something else that I chanced upon him. One day, while searching through those large books at the Family Records Centre, I came across a James Handsford in the death records. Something seemed to ring a bell. On the spur of the moment, I decided to blow £7 on ordering the death certificate. My hunch turned out to be correct. The certificate revealed that he died on 27 January 1923 in Prestwich lunatic asylum. Prestwich is close to Manchester and a little distance from Wigan. The occupation is given as 'labourer', and the cause of death as 'chronic renal disease of some years and fatty heart of some years'. A post mortem was not required. No family members are mentioned on the document; the informant was the medical superintendent of the asylum. The only clue on the certificate to a connection with the family is an address: 5 Miry Lane, Wigan. The family home was at number 4, but this was too big a coincidence to ignore. The age – 57 – is slightly incorrect: it should be 59. All this appears to indicate a certain separation from family. Our ancestors were not as tolerant of mental illness or learning disability as we are today. To have a member of the family suffer this misfortune was sometimes difficult to cope with. It was a stigma that in many cases was kept a family secret.

Was James John placed in a lunatic asylum and forgotten about? It is quite possible. We have to remember that his father died in 1903, and his mother in 1913. About the time James John disappeared, his parents would have been in their fifties and perhaps no longer able to cope with an adult son with a mental disability. What is certain is that James John's nephews and nieces appeared to be completely unaware of his existence. If they did know about him, they kept it a secret. Neither my father nor my aunts ever mentioned him within my hearing. What was related to me on one occasion by a family member, however, was that my aunts 'had a horror of' lunatic asylums. Was poor James John the reason? It may well be the case.

### ELIZABETH REYNOLDS HANSFORD 1866-?

Elizabeth Reynolds was born on 6 June 1866. The family were now back in Chatham, living in Henry Street. Her parents followed the common Victorian custom of linking her name to that of another relative. In this case her second name was her mother's maiden name.

On 27 April 1889, Elizabeth married James Collier, a painter from Wigan and the son of Miles Collier, also a painter. The marriage took place in the church of St Thomas, Wigan.

*James and Elizabeth (Lily) Collier. It is quite possible that this was a wedding photograph.*

*The interior of St Thomas's church Wigan*

My father had mentioned a Lily Collier when I was jotting down my original notes. I searched in vain for such a person, until I realised that Lily must have been Elizabeth's nickname. I have a photograph that shows the young couple posing for the camera – a photograph taken, I imagine, round about the time of their wedding. It may even be a wedding photograph.

It took a long time to substantiate my father's statement that he thought James and Lily had gone to America.. Certainly in 1901 the couple were still in Wigan. On the census for that year they both appear as visitors at the house of Elizabeth's younger sister Harriet Georgina and her husband, William Warden. The purpose of the visit may have been to see the new baby, who was just 5 days old.

The eagerly awaited 1911 census was of no help. I could not find James and Elizabeth on it.

It was my cousin who provided a breakthrough in the form of a US passport application for a James Collier (father Miles Collier, deceased) to visit England in 1920. The document indicates that he had originally arrived in the USA in 1907.

James travelled to England in May 1920 and returned to the USA in August of the same year. Was there a special reason for his visit? It seems likely. Elizabeth's sister Harriet Georgina, by then a widow, emigrated to the USA in February 1921. On 11 March 1921 she married James Collier, widower.

All this confirms my father's statement that the Colliers, or at least one of them, went to

America. But what happened to Elizabeth (Lily) Collier? Did she go to America with her husband and die young? It looks as if this may have been the case. Hopefully more detailed research of US records may throw some light on the intriguing questions this new information raises.

## FREDERICK EDWIN HANSFORD 1869-1923

Frederick Edwin was born on 13 February 1869. By this time the family had moved to Loose, on the outskirts of Maidstone.

In his early working life Frederick appears to have followed the pattern of many similar young men by taking up employment in the cotton industry. The 1891 census shows him aged 22, employed as a cotton carder. He was still following this occupation at the time of the 1901 census. Unusually for the period, he was still unmarried at the age of 32.

This was to change on 23 December 1914, when Frederick married Mary Alice Challender at St Bartholomew's church, Westhoughton. Westhoughton is a small town between Wigan and Bolton. Frederick would have been 45 then, and the First World War had just started.

It is interesting that in the period between the 1901 census and the time of his marriage, Frederick changed his occupation. On his marriage certificate he stated that he was a hairdresser. He gave his address as Market Street, Westhoughton. Mary gave hers as King Street, Westhoughton.

On 20 June 1918 their son George Wilfred was born at 59 Market Street. Once again, Frederick's occupation was given as a hairdresser, but now he was also a tobacconist. I imagine that he had a small shop with a gents' hairdressing salon in the back room, like hundreds of similar establishments of the time.

On 4 June 1923 Frederick died from septic meningitis, leaving Mary to bring up their 5-year-old son. At the time of his death he kept a sweet and tobacco shop at 57 Market Street, Westhoughton. The informant's name on the death certificate is Elizabeth Challender, Frederick's sister-in-law.

Tragedy was to overtake the family again in 1934. On 19 March George Wilfred died at the age of 15 in Bolton Royal Infirmary from appendicitis with complications. Coincidentally, his cousin George, ordained in the Church of England, was chaplain to Bolton Royal Infirmary at the time. My cousin Mildred remembers going to George Wilfred's funeral in Westhoughton. By all accounts he had been a promising musician.

## FANNY ADA CHARLOTTE HANSFORD 1870-1930

Fanny Ada Charlotte was born on 6 September 1870. The family were still living in Loose, Maidstone at the time, but no address appears on her birth certificate. Harriet Eliza, who registered the birth on 17 October, gave her husband's occupation as 'engine smith'. This was the second time she had recorded this information, so clearly by this time Thomas Henry had developed his skills in metal working into a more specialised domain.

Fanny would have been perhaps only 5 or 6 years old when the family moved to Wigan. She would have had only vague memories of life in Kent. She would have gone to school and grown up experiencing only life in the industrial north of England. Unlike many local women of her age, she did not go to work in the cotton mills. The 1901 census lists her as a domestic servant. By that time she and her brother Frederick were the only two children in the family living at home with their aged parents.

On 6 April 1904, nine months after the death of her father, Fanny married Henry Fair, a 36-year-old widower who worked as a sanitary inspector, in the church of St Thomas, where most of Fanny's brothers and sisters had been married. At the time the family were still living at 4 Miry Lane.

On 13 August 1905, at their home, 22 Gidlow Lane, Wigan, Fanny gave birth to their son, Henry. It is my understanding that it was Harry, as he was known, who investigated the will that left a legacy to the Hansford family, about which I have written more in the section of this book entitled Exploring the Family Legends.

Fanny died of cancer on 18 October 1930, survived by her husband Henry, now widowed for the second time.

Six years after Fanny's death, her son Harry, then aged 31 and a motor mechanic, married shorthand typist Annie Thomas on 19 December 1936, in St George's church, Wigan.

## HARRIET GEORGINA HANSFORD 1872-?

Harriet Georgina was Thomas Henry and Harriet Eliza's last registered child. By the time she was born, her mother was 40 years old and had been rearing children for nearly twenty years. According to available records, she had given birth to eleven children.

By the time of Harriet Georgina's birth, Thomas Henry had moved his family back to London. They must have just moved, because in the 1871 census they were still living in

Loose. Instead of returning to Chatham or Greenwich, however, the family took up residence in Newington. The registration of the birth took place in the district of St Saviours, which included Bermonsey, Lambeth, Newington, St Olave and Southwark.

Clearly it was work that had taken Thomas Henry back to London. It is possible that he was already familiar with this area; his marriage twenty years previously had taken place in Waterloo, part of nearby Lambeth.

Harriet Georgina was born on 18 January 1872. The family at the time would have consisted of Mary Ann, at 15 the eldest child in the household, William Charles, aged 14, Caroline Elizabeth, aged 12, Charles Saunders, aged 10, James John, aged 8, Elizabeth Reynolds, aged 6, Frederick Edwin, age 3, and Fanny, not yet 2 years old.

Harriet Georgina would still have been a young child when the family moved north. Like her sister Fanny and brother Frederick, she would grow up in Wigan with little or no recollection of life anywhere else. By this time school was compulsory, so with her brother and sisters she would have received a basic education.

On 27 November 1895, Harriet Georgina married William Warden, a widower who had his own business as a blacksmith. William was 31 at the time of their marriage, and Harriet Georgina was 23. Frederick and Fanny were the witnesses.

The couple appear on the 1901 census living at 14, Sharp Street, Wigan. It looks as if they had three children by this time: William, aged 1, Alice, just 5 days old, and Annie, aged 3, who spent the night of the census with her grandparents at 4 Miry Lane. Sadly, Annie died in the same year and was buried on 25 October in Wigan cemetery, in a plot that had been purchased by her father.

On the 1911 census the Wardens were living at 173 Ormskirk Road, Pemberton, Wigan. Listed are William, aged 47, a 'shoeing smith', Harriet Georgina, aged 39, and their children William, aged 11, Florence, aged 10, and Evelyn, aged 4. Despite exhaustive searches, no further record of Alice has so far come to light.

Tragedy visited the family again shortly afterwards, for William Warden died and was buried on 7 June 1911 next to his little daughter Annie.

It appears that Harriet Georgina had the will and the ability to carry on her husband's business. There is evidence that she ran it right up until about 1920, when her life was again to change dramatically. She sold the business. This decision may have been dictated by several factors. The mainstay of the business appears to have been shoeing horses. With the end of the First World War, cars were beginning to make an impact. Though there were still horses requiring shoes, it was clearly a diminishing market. There was also another reason.

In May 1920 Harriet Georgina's brother-in-law, James Collier, arrived from America.

His wife, Lily, had died, and on the 1920 American census he had described himself as a widower. He stayed in Wigan until July of that year, when he returned to America.

Did he propose marriage to his sister-in-law during that visit, or had an agreement been made between them beforehand? We cannot be sure. However, what is certain is that the following February Harriet Georgina was on her way to America, where she married James a few weeks later. Listed with her on the passenger manifest of the SS *Cedric* were her children William, aged 21, 'laborer', Florence, aged 19, 'domestic', Evelyn aged 14, also described as a domestic, and Frank, aged 9.

The 1930 census for the USA shows James Collier, painter, living with his wife Harriet and his two stepchildren Evelyn and Frank in University City, St Louis, Missouri.

# WILLIAM CHARLES HANSFORD 1858-1926

I never met my paternal grandfather. He died nine years and my grandmother three years before I was born, so both my grandparents were mysterious figures to me. My father rarely talked about his family, but I can recall that on one occasion, when I was perhaps 6 or 7 years old and my father was watching me fiddling intently with some bolts and nuts, he remarked, 'You are going to be an engineer. Your grandfather was an engineer.' It was from that kind of comment that I built up a picture of my grandparents. However, it was from family history research that I composed a wider picture and provided a framework for those snippets of information.

William Charles Hansford was born in Best Street, Chatham, on 3 December 1858. The name sounds odd at first, but it is nothing to do with being the best street in the town: it is named after James Best (1720-82), a local businessman and benefactor. The street, which was not far away from the High Street, was composed of terraced houses popular for

*William Charles Hansford 1858–1926*

88

*Best Street Chatham about 1900*

rented accommodation. It would have been well known to Thomas Henry Hansford when he moved his family back to Chatham, as various other members of the family had lived there. Today there are no longer any houses in Best Street. The ones in which Thomas Henry and his family lived were pulled down in 1935 and the once-quiet street now serves as a busy relief road around the town. A photograph taken before all the buildings were demolished shows rows of timber-fronted houses with entrances immediately off the narrow pavement. Only a few modern commercial buildings now mark the spot where the little community of houses once stood.

Queen Victoria had already been on the throne of England for twenty years when William was born. Parts of England had changed from a rural environment to an industrial one. The Lancashire cotton mills, which would provide work for William and his family, were already well established, and rows of small houses had grown up around the mills to house the workers.

When Thomas Henry moved his family to Wigan in the 1870s, the town had become a busy industrial centre. The population had almost tripled from around 11,000 at the beginning of the 19th century to about 32,000 fifty years later. This rapid increase was mainly due to the expansion of industry. The cotton mills, coal mines and engineering factories attracted workers to the town.

Thomas Henry and Harriet Eliza's family at that time consisted of ten children, and William Charles would have been 16 or 17. He probably already had several years' work experience.

*Mary Hansford (Worthington)*

William Charles found employment in Victoria Mills. It is difficult to establish what job he actually did. The 1881 census describes his occupation as 'overlooker', which was a term for a supervisor. I always had the impression that he was involved in the engineering side of the industry. This may have been so. Information given to the census enumerator was not always completely accurate. Our Victorian ancestors disliked official forms just as much as we do today.

On 29 July 1885 William Charles married Mary Worthington in the church of St Thomas, Wigan. He was then 27; Mary was 23 and the second daughter of George and Margaret Worthington, an established Wigan family. On Mary's birth certificate her father's occupation appears as 'iron moulder'.

William Charles and Mary's first child, Caroline, was born on 17 May 1886. The couple were then living at Frith Street, Wigan.

Their second child, George, was born on 16 May 1889. By then the family had moved to Warrington Road, Pemberton, a district of Wigan. William Charles, who registered the birth of his son, gave his occupation as 'cotton carder'.

By the time their second daughter, Mary, was born, on 7 December 1892, William Charles had moved his family to Golborne, a village on the outskirts of Wigan. The name Golborne means 'golden stream' or 'stream where marsh marigolds grow'. Today Golborne is still quite a rural area of Wigan, with a pub and houses nestling together. This move may have been in connection with William Charles's work; on Mary's birth certificate he describes himself once again as an overlooker in a cotton factory.

A third daughter, Nellie, was born on 22 May 1895. Sadly, she lived for less than two years. She died on 5 November 1896 and was buried in a corner of Golborne churchyard.

The next child born to William Charles and Mary was my father, Thomas, on 18 April 1898; the family were still living in Golborne, in Bank Street, which is still in existence.

After my father, my grandparents had two more daughters: Annie, born on 21 September 1901, and Lily, born 6 April 1904. By this time the family of eight had moved to 119 Gidlow Lane, Wigan, an address they were to occupy for a few years. Although during this period my grandfather continued to describe his occupation as 'overlooker' or, more often, 'cotton carder', it seems that he and my grandmother were also becoming more and more involved in the grocery business. This would have been a logical step to take, because the Worthington family had a background in similar small businesses.

In the early years of the new century, my grandparents moved to 4 Lorne Street, in a quiet neighbourhood of terraced houses on hilly ground perhaps twenty minutes' walk from the centre of Wigan. It was there that they started a grocery shop in what would have been the converted front room of the house, presumably run by my grandmother, perhaps with help from her family. The shop served the local community for a few years, but its eventual change of direction was dictated by the economic situation. For the working population of that time, money was short, and this was often made worse by lay-offs and strikes, and possibly by the tendency of some family breadwinners to spend too much money in the public house. In this difficult situation, in order to put some sort of meal on the table housewives would ask the local shopkeeper if they could have some groceries 'on tick', meaning that they would pay at the end of the week when the wages came in. The problem was that quite often at the end of the week there was little change in the family's finances, so once again the shopkeeper lost out and the money owed got larger. To move away from this type of business, the tiny shop in Lorne Street was turned into a bakery cum confectionery'. This was a logical choice: my grandmother's sister Elizabeth, whom my father referred to as 'Auntie Lizzie', already ran a confectionery shop in Queen Street. No doubt she was able to give her younger sister valuable advice on the running of such an establishment. I remember visiting and staying at 4 Lorne Street in the 1950s and witnessing at first hand the produce of the tiny business run by my aunts Caroline and Lily, known in my family as Auntie Carrie and Auntie Lily. Each day delicious meat pies would be baked and put out for sale in the shop around midday, piping hot from the oven. My aunts also used to make the most delicious vanilla slices. I have never tasted any quite like them.

William Charles died at 4 Lorne Street on 31 October 1926. The cause of death was given as bronchitis and cardiac syncope (loss of consciousness due to a heart problem).

It is difficult to know what kind of man my grandfather was, but it is possible to get some idea from the odd comment picked up here and there. Certainly he appears to have been a very hard-working and industrious husband and father. He also appears to have had a gentler side to him. He affectionately used to call my grandmother 'Polly' and I am told that it was his practice to take the left-over fancy breads and cakes from the shop to work, where they were eagerly devoured by the hungry mill girls. Despite the description of his job in the various documents available, like his father he must have had a leaning towards engineering, because my father once told me that he had a small lathe in his back shed that he worked on in his spare time.

With William Charles's passing, another family link with the Victorian age ended. My grandfather lived through many changes. When he was a young man and first came to Wigan the horse and carriage were the vogue, and the nation's railway system was still developing. He would have seen the coming of the motor car and the aeroplane, and he would have been aware of the horrors and trauma of the First World War, as it affected citizens in Britain more than any other war until then. In the town of Wigan much had happened since his arrival in the 1870s. The new market hall was built in 1877, and Mesnes Park was laid out and opened a year later, quickly followed by a public library. Electric trams ran in the streets for the first time in 1901. William Charles would have witnessed all these events.

Mary, my grandmother, survived my grandfather for six years. She died at 4 Lorne Street on 31 March 1932. Her will reveals that she owned a few small properties in Queen Street, Wigan, an area of the town where her family's roots lay.

# THE CHILDREN OF WILLIAM CHARLES HANSFORD
# AND MARY WORTHINGTON

### CAROLINE HANSFORD 1886-1969

Caroline was William Charles and Mary's first child. She was born on 17 May 1886, just ten months after their marriage.

I met my aunt Caroline on several occasions in my younger years. My impression of her as a teenager was of a rather overweight woman who seemed quite stern at times.

When I knew her, she ran the confectionery shop in Lorne Street with her younger sister Lily, turning out each day the delicious meat pies for which they had a local reputation. I remember during a brief stay there helping them in the tiny bakehouse in the yard at the rear of the house, and in the shop at their peak selling period around midday. At times I thought Auntie Carrie (Caroline) was also a bit blunt in her dealings with customers, all of whom she knew well. However, this might just have been the impression of a young person from outside who was unused to the Lancashire way of speaking.

From my limited observation of my two aunts it appeared that Caroline was the leading partner in the business and that she tended to enjoy this role.

Caroline died from a coronary thrombosis in The Royal Albert Edward Infirmary, Wigan, on 8 October 1969.

From a family history point of view, with her passing a great opportunity was lost. Caroline and Lily held the family history knowledge and, sadly, many of the loose ends and questions generated by my research could have been tied up if my aunts had been around when I began.

### GEORGE HANSFORD 1889-1974

I never met my uncle George. William Charles and Mary's first son, he came into this world

*George Hansford 1889-1974*

on 16 May 1889 at 88 Warrington Road, Newtown, Pemberton, Wigan. Pemberton is a suburb of Wigan and the family was probably living there as a result of William Charles's work as a cotton carder in the mills.

Not a lot is known about George's early life. It is to be assumed that he went to school and did the usual things boys of that period did. Auntie Carrie and her sister Lily appeared to have great admiration for him, certainly in later years.

Directly opposite the family home in 4 Lorne Street stands the majestic building of St Catherine's church, its spire recognisable from quite a distance. Sadly, the clock that used to boom out the time on every quarter-hour is now silent. It was in this church that George in his late teens heard the call to holy orders, while standing under one of the windows in the church observing the sunlight streaming through. So strong was his conviction to become a priest that from that moment on George focused his energy on attaining his ambition.

On 2 April 1917 George married Edith Critchley in St Catherine's church. By this time he was a member of the Church Army and his occupation on the marriage certificate appears as 'evangelist'. Thomas, George's younger brother and my father, was one of the witnesses.

Edith was to prove an admirable support for the young clergyman, even being the main breadwinner for them at one stage while her husband completed his studies. George studied at St Paul's Missionary College, Burgh le Marsh, near Skegness, Lincolnshire, set up in 1878 to train students for foreign missionary work. In 1919 he passed his 1st Theological Examination and took up the position of curate at a church in Newark. He was ordained a priest on 19 December 1920 in Southwell Minster.

In 1924 George undertook missionary work in British Guiana. It was to prove a disastrous mistake. The harsh climate did not suit him and he quickly went down with a fever. A move to a cooler environment was necessary for his health. In 1926 the couple returned to England, poorer and wiser. It is highly likely that, because George did not complete his period of missionary work, they had to pay their own passage home. Edith was once heard to remark that they came back to England penniless and had only the clothes they stood up in.

Following this interlude, George was curate at the parish church of All Saints in Wigan until he became vicar of New Bury, Bolton in 1927. He was also chaplain to Bolton Royal Infirmary, where in 1934 he had the sad duty of attending the bedside of his cousin George Wilfred, who died of appendicitis aged just 15.

My uncle's dedication to the church continued throughout his life. He held a number of posts as vicar, mostly in Lancashire, Nottinghamshire and Lincolnshire. In 1945 he returned to Wigan to become vicar of St Andrew's church. Despite occasionally meeting resistance to his chosen path from people who had known him before he entered the Church, he proved in general to be a well-respected and popular vicar.

By all accounts George was a retiring man who was devoted to his vocation, which he carried out to the best of his ability. Edith was always supportive, though the general opinion in the family was that she often assumed the role of decision maker for matters in their lives that were unconnected with the Church.

Sadly George and Edith never had any children to fulfil their lives. Edith gave birth to two babies, but they did not survive.

George and Edith always gave the appearance of careful and modest living. My uncle was once heard to remark that they had disposed of their car because it was a luxury they could not afford.

When George's career came to an end, he and Edith retired to Dulverton Hall, a residence for retired clergy in St Martin's Square, Scarborough. However, their stay there was brief. Their next move was to Fosbrooke House in Lytham St Annes, a retirement development for Church of England clergy. This was followed by a flat in Bolton, owned by a Dr Smith who was a lifelong friend of George's. Their last recorded residence was again Dulverton Hall in Scarborough.

George died of a coronary thrombosis in Clifton Hospital, York on 17 August 1974. Shortly before his death he was heard to remark, 'It will be the 17th,' clearly referring to his departure from this world.

## The ministry of George Hansford

1908/9-1915/16         Church Army

| | |
|---|---|
| [dates unknown] | St Paul's Missionary College |
| 1919 | 1st Theological Examination |
| 1919-22 | Curate of Newark |
| 1920 | Ordained a priest in Southwell Minster |
| 1922-24 | Armadale Mission and Bathgate, Linlithgow, Falkirk |
| 1924-25 | Missionary to Makusi Indians, Rupununi, British Guiana |
| 1925-26 | St John's, Bartica, British Guiana |
| 1927 | Curate of All Saints, Wigan |
| 1927-36 | New Bury, Bolton |
| 1936-43 | Beeston |
| 1943-45 | Tuxford |
| 1945-50 | St Andrew's, Wigan |
| 1950-53 | Belton, Isle of Axholme |
| 1953-56 | Carlton Le Moorland and Stapleford |
| 1956-59 | Anderby and Cumberworth |
| 1962 | Dulverton Hall, Scarborough |

## MARY HANSFORD 1892-1968

By the time Mary was born on 7 December 1892, William Charles and Mary already had Caroline, aged 6, and George, aged 3, running around at their family home in Golborne, a village on the outskirts of Wigan.

Of all the members of my father's immediate family, my aunt Mary is the one about whom I know the least. I met her only once, and the impression I took away was of a pleasant and friendly hard-working wife and mother.

Like many young women, Mary enjoyed dancing and it was at a local dance that she met Alfred Carter, who at the time was working as a miner. The friendship flourished and on 24 September 1921 the couple were married in St Catherine's church, Wigan. Mary was 28 at the time, and Alfred 30. The marriage ceremony was performed by Mary's brother George, who had been ordained a priest the year before.

Mary and Alfred had two children, Mildred and Ronald. Mildred was born in 1925, and Ronald in 1929.

At times the marriage was dogged by Alfred's ill health, the result of being exposed to gas in the First World War and from working in the mines. Despite these limitations, he did not let them interfere with providing for his family. I met him briefly in the 1950s and he appeared to be a man who could adapt quite easily, seeking employment where it could be found. He also helped in the family confectionery business until the flour started to irritate the skin problem that was the legacy of his exposure to gas in the First World War.

Mary was very supportive, working when she could to provide extra income for the family. My mother once remarked to me that she felt sorry for Auntie Mary because she had experienced a hard life, and certainly she and her family had their fair share of difficulties to overcome.

Alfred died on 17 August 1956 and Mary survived him by another 12 years. Mary died in hospital from a coronary thrombosis on 29 November 1968.

### NELLIE HANSFORD 1895-1896

Nellie was born on 22 May 1895, while the family were living in Golborne. She had a very short life: she died on 5 November 1896. The cause of death was recorded as 'tonsillitis (3 days) and parotitis (5 days)', parotitis being inflammation of the salivary glands. Such a sudden death from what these days is considered a comparatively mild complaint contrasts with the advances of medical science and the availability of modern treatment. Nellie is buried in a corner of St Thomas's churchyard, Golborne.

### THOMAS HANSFORD 1898-1965

A comprehensive account of the life of Thomas Hansford, my father, appears under a separate heading.

### ANNIE HANSFORD 1901-1972

Annie was born on 21 September 1901, while the family were living at 119 Gidlow Lane, Wigan.

On 30 May 1939 she married Horace Grounds Bannister, a local engineer, at the parish church of All Saints in Wigan. The marriage service was carried out by the bride's brother George, and Annie's sisters Caroline and Lily were the witnesses. Both Horace and Annie were committed members of their local church throughout their lives.

Annie and Horace had one child, born in 1942 – a wartime baby. By this time Horace was too old for military service.

Annie died from a coronary thrombosis at her home in Wigan on 2 June 1972, and Horace lived on to the ripe old age of 92. He died in 1987.


**LILY HANSFORD 1904-1991**


Lily was William Charles and Mary's seventh and last child. She was born on 6 April 1904, while the family were still living at Gidlow Lane.

Lily would have been very much the 'baby' of the family. Her eldest sister Caroline would have been 18 when she was born, and her brother George 15. Even her other sister Mary would have reached the age of 12. The children in the family closest in age to her would have been my father, Thomas, aged 6, and Annie, who was just 3 when Lily was born.

Perhaps this is why these three always appeared to have a close affinity with each other. My father once remarked that he always got on very well with his young sister Lily.

No details appear to exist to indicate whether Lily was trained for any particular job. In later life, she lived with her oldest unmarried sister, Caroline, at 4 Lorne Street, their parents' home, and ran the confectionery shop there until 1964, when she retired at the age of 60. Like her sister, she remained unmarried. She was once overheard to remark that the reason why so many women of her generation remained single was the decimation of the male population during the First World War.

During her life and partnership with Caroline, Lily appeared to accept her older sister's lead, particularly in the running of the business, and she seemed to be quite happy with this arrangement. At one stage, she was in favour of moving the business to larger and better premises; Caroline, however, was not happy with the suggestion and the idea was dropped.

Lily took an active interest in the children of her sisters Mary and Annie. She would take them out for the day and on at least one occasion she took them on holiday.

Like several of the female members of the Hansford family of her generation, Lily tended to put on weight and became quite stout in later years.

She died of heart disease on 26 June 1991 at the age of 87.

# THOMAS HANSFORD 1898-1965

Thomas, my father, was the second of William Charles and Mary's two sons. He was born on 18 April 1898 at Bank Street, Golborn. He appeared not to think too highly of being born in this area of Wigan, but I never found out why.

After leaving school, he went to work in the engineering industry. He attempted to educate himself further by going to evening classes at Wigan Mining and Technical College. He once told me the story of a teacher in one class he went to who tended to have favourite students. One in particular was always praised highly. My father with his limited education struggled amid such expertise, and one evening the teacher remarked sarcastically that perhaps it would be best if he concentrated his efforts on the practical work and left the academic work to others. However, my father must have been determined, because a little later his results were better than those of the teacher's favourite. Even this was used to effect by the teacher. When my father arrived a few minutes late for class one evening, the

*Thomas Hansford  1898-1965*

same teacher with the same sarcasm remarked, 'Now the important people are here, we will start.'

When my father was 18 he fell sick with rheumatic fever. Unfortunately, the illness was not recognised at first by the doctor treating him, with the result that his heart was permanently damaged. He was unable to return to his previous work and received little sympathy from his family, who appeared to consider that this was the end of his working life. However, through sheer determination Thomas struggled back to some sort of normality. He managed to find work in the theatre in the evenings, shifting scenery. He met many of the old-time music hall stars.

My father would have liked to become a chemist. He did all the preparatory work, up to the stage when he would have had to commence specialised training. Sadly, his hopes of continuing were dashed. His parents announced that they had no money available to help him finance his studies. It was a blow that my father felt very badly, particularly as his brother George had followed his chosen profession, presumably with some support from their parents. My father felt that he had been treated badly, considering what he had so far achieved. It also meant he had to think about another way to earn a living

Gradually he found his way into the building industry. This was how he met my mother. My understanding is that he was working as a joiner in the area in which she lived: Oulton, near Leeds. This is what my parents told me. However, my cousins in Wigan are convinced that my parents met as a result of my maternal grandfather's employment as a gardener at Haigh Hall in Wigan; they insist that their first meeting took place during one of my mother's visits to her father. While there may be an element of truth in this story, I am convinced that they first met in Yorkshire, not Lancashire.

*Mildred Hansford (Hutchinson)*

My parents were married in Oulton parish church on 21 March 1925. My mother's father, William Hutchinson, and my father's sister Annie were the witnesses. My mother once told me that she got married very early in the morning, around breakfast time, and that the parson who conducted the service was blind. At the time, my mother was working as a bookkeeper in the wholesale drapery trade, in an establishment in Leeds called Batty's.

My parents moved into accommodation rented by my father at Malton, a small town north of York. My mother once commented that cement dust rose in clouds from the floor every time she attempted to sweep it.

A male child was born to my parents around 1926, sadly stillborn. At the time there was no requirement to register stillborn babies, so no records have been revealed. It seems that my parents were living in Oulton at the time, as my brother is convinced that the child is buried in Oulton, at St John's parish church. However, the church does not appear to have any record of the burial.

My brother, Kenneth Leslie, was born on 30 May 1927. The address was given as Farrar Lane, Oulton, which was my grandparents' home.

Sometime in the early 1930s, my father obtained a job in the building department on the estate of the Duke of Richmond at Goodwood, near Chichester. This was promotion for him: a move from manual to white-collar work. However, my mother did not like life in Sussex; she always remarked that the air did not suit her – whatever that meant. It was perhaps this that prompted my father to seek work elsewhere. Opportunity was to come up in the form of the position of clerk of works at Dartington, in Devon, where Leonard and Dorothy Elmhirst had purchased the run-down estate in 1925 and started a school in the old buildings.

My father was by all accounts somewhat apprehensive about taking this position, unsure whether he had the necessary skills. I think he was encouraged by his boss at Goodwood, who in reply to his concerns remarked: 'Hansford, it is not what you know but what you pretend you know that is important.' In spite of his concerns, my father appears to have made a success of the job, and the family enjoyed the most positive and productive time of their lives during their five-year stay at Dartington.

I was born in 1935, and shortly afterwards we moved into a brand-new house in Dartington called Lyndene, which my father had built with the help of a small legacy from his mother, who had died in 1932. My father was supplied with a car for his work and we also had a telephone in the house – definitely middle-class possessions in the 1930s. My father involved himself in the social life at Dartington Hall and met many people who would later become quite well known in various artistic fields.

The Second World War was to bring this lifestyle to an abrupt end. In the early days of the war, uncertainty was the watchword. Nobody knew how things would turn out. It was my mother who instigated the family's next move. She had lived through the dropping of bombs on the town of Sheffield in the First World War, and the scenes she had witnessed remained with her as traumatic memories. One night in the early days of the war, an allied bomber laden with bombs crashed close to our home. The explosions woke my mother, and memories of the First World War came back to her. As a result my parents decided to make a move to what they considered a safer place to bring up my brother and me.

The Isle of Man was chosen as the destination. My father had spent a holiday there with his aunts at a very young age, and it must have made quite an impression on him. My mother moved there first with my brother and me. My father arrived unexpectedly a few weeks later. It was a strange transformation from the lush Devonshire countryside to the rather bleaker island landscape.

As his heart condition exempted him from military service, my father joined the Air Ministry. For a short period he was involved in surveying work for the aircraft navigation system known as beam approach.

At the end of the war he resigned from the Air Ministry. It had been the general consensus between my mother, my brother and me that our stay on the Isle of Man would be only for the period of the war. My father, however, did not seem to share this viewpoint. As a result the family remained there for the next fifteen years. My father had a number of jobs both on the Isle of Man and in England, most of fairly short duration. I never recall him being in a job for much longer than twelve months during this time. He usually told my mother after he had resigned. At one point he worked abroad for short periods, including the Bahamas, Jamaica and East Africa. When he was unemployed, it was my mother who kept the home together and paid the bills with the proceeds of a small poultry farm she started in the field at the back of the house.

It was my brother and I who perhaps were the catalyst for a change of location. We both found it impossible to obtain work on the Isle of Man and were forced to return to England.

In 1960 my parents sold up and moved back to England permanently, first to Leeds, where my mother had relatives, and then to Winsford, a small town not far from Crewe. The move to Winsford was to prove disastrous. My father's health was deteriorating, but in spite of this he insisted on renovating the bungalow he and my mother had purchased, on his own and without any help. It is possible that this aggravated his heart condition and caused his sudden death on 16 November 1965 only a few months after they had moved into their new home. He was cremated and his ashes interred in Crewe cemetery. Of his brothers and sisters, only Annie and Lily came to the funeral, together with my mother, my sister-in-law Doreen, my brother and me.

My mother eventually sold the bungalow and moved back to Leeds to live with her sister. She died suddenly in Leeds General Infirmary on 15 January 1971, after being taken ill only hours previously.

What sort of man was my father? I think the events of his early life created a hurt that he would not acknowledge, even to himself. I think inwardly he felt cheated in life. A wrong diagnosis had ruined his health, but despite this he had clawed his way back to his chosen career, only to be denied help by his parents. His feelings of resentment may have been deepened by the likelihood that his older brother had received help from their parents to become a parson. There certainly appeared to be some sort of rift between the two brothers, though my father never admitted it. In many ways, he always appeared to be estranged from his family, though his sisters clearly thought the world of him. After he married my mother, my father did not have a great deal of contact with his family; perhaps he only saw them when he was passing through Wigan on his way somewhere.

It is also quite possible that throughout his life my father felt insecure, particular in the area of employment. He was conscious that he was largely self-taught. He never liked to be away from his job for any length of time and I can recall that one of the few family holidays we had was cut short by my father wishing to return to work for some reason.

Socially, my father was definitely the more extrovert of my parents. Although my mother would welcome the few guests who came to our house, and they appeared to enjoy coming, it was my father who tended naturally to befriend people. When we were living at Dartington, he would be out every evening. My mother once commented that the only time he ever spent an evening at home was when he damaged his ribs and movement was painful. She, on the other hand, rarely went out to social events.

My recollection of my father as a manager was that he was extremely popular with the workforce. He had the respect and admiration of those under him, perhaps because he spoke their language and did not talk down to them. I can recall in my early working life conversations with people who had worked under him or who had had close contact with him at work, and they appeared to have great admiration and respect for him.

On the downside, he was easily taken in. He would frequently be befriended by someone who wanted a job done and knew my father could do it but would then let him down by not paying for the completed work. When that happened, he would say to my mother, who had seen the true situation from the start, 'You were right.'

Generous, he would give away or share many of the possessions he had struggled to acquire, often to unappreciative recipients. In later life, when he and my mother were no longer affluent, he would sometimes draw up plans for someone who intended to do some building but rather than hiring an expensive architect would ask my father to do the job. He would charge a very low rate and then refuse to ask for the money when the bill remained unpaid. On the few occasions when he was paid, he would immediately give the money to another member of the family for something they wanted or needed, regardless of the fact that he himself might have been in need of a new item of clothing.

In many ways my father was a kind of Sydney Carton character. In business he would work in the background helping others achieve the limelight and prosperity. It never occurred to him that he could have done the same for himself and his family. However, it has to be said that he was not very skilled in financial matters. He lacked the ability to keep track of money, and he rarely managed to save. It was my mother who handled all the family's finances. During the period immediately after the war, when my father was forced to take employment in England, he spent his hard-earned money on lodgings. It never seemed to occur to him that it might have been more productive and economical to move his family to where he found work.

This was another strange thing about my father. He sometimes appeared to want to keep his family isolated. He would often choose somewhere to live that was miles from anywhere, much to my mother's disapproval.

I think he would have liked to embark on a *Moon and Sixpence* existence. The thought of living a primitive life definitely appealed to him.

In many ways my father was not a family man. I can only recall his once offering to come and play a game of cricket with my brother and me, and that was brought abruptly to an end after two minutes' play when he sent a ball through the kitchen window...

However, on the plus side he had an immense knowledge of things: when I expressed an interest in the stars, he spent quite a long time pointing out the various constellations and planets in the heavens. Ask him anything, and I have little doubt that he would have been able to provide an answer. I remember he encouraged me to take up painting at an early age. He had himself learnt to paint during his stay at Dartington, when he mixed with some of the artists who frequently visited the school. A great reader, he always had a vast stock of books around him, usually kept in rather untidy shelves, because he was not the neatest of men.

He never seemed to care a great deal about his appearance. Being tall and lanky he would have benefited from a smart turnout, but on the whole he preferred to rely on well-worn clothes rather than using up the suits he kept carefully folded in suitcases and rarely wore, much to my mother's dismay. Right until the end of his life, he insisted on wearing starched detachable collars instead of modern shirts with attached soft collars. On the other hand, he always liked my mother to dress up – a strange contrast!

Perhaps my father can be summed up by a remark made recently by somebody who knew him reasonably well: 'He was quite a character.'

# WILLIAM EDWARD HANSFORD 1878-1918

William Hansford (his second name, Edward, does not appear on his birth certificate*) was born in Chatham on 9 August 1878. His parents are recorded as William Archer, chimney sweep, and Eleanor Archer, formerly Hansford. Eleanor was James senior's great-granddaughter via his daughter Amelia. I have never discovered any marriage for William Archer and Eleanor Hansford; it would appear to have been a common-law arrangement. After William died in 1888 at the age of 28, Eleanor reverted to her maiden name.

With the early and tragic death of her partner, Eleanor was left with five children to bring up. One can only imagine the struggle she must have had. The living conditions of the poor at the time were extremely bad. If Eleanor did manage to find any work to support her family, it would have been hard for her children. While she was out at work the children may well have had to fend for themselves; the older children would have had to look after the younger ones, possibly against a miserable background of hunger and inadequate living accommodation. Very often children in such circumstances were themselves forced to work or beg and scavenge for food. Photographs of the period depict malnourished children, unshod and dressed in whatever clothes they could find and with a look of resignation on their faces. It would be in conditions of this kind that Eleanor's children grew up.

Within six months of her partner's death Eleanor was forced to give up the struggle and seek the assistance of that last resort for the poor: the workhouse. On 22 May 1889, she and her five children were admitted to Medway Union Workhouse. Being 11 years old at the

*A question mark hangs over William's second name. I can find no trace of it on early records. When I first came across him on naval records, my immediate thought that he was not part of my family, because I had no William Edward listed. Eleanor's son was simply baptised William. However, after more detailed research, I am convinced that the William Edward Hansford appearing on naval records is the William Hansford who was sent to a naval training ship for boys from Medway Union Workhouse. Dates, places, the names of relatives and the ages of people involved all match. For some reason the name Edward was adopted during his naval career.

time, William would have been fully able to comprehend his new status.

It was against this background that he grew into his teens. He would have received some schooling during this period, as well as carrying out the tedious tasks of the workhouse. It is highly likely that he was separated from his mother and sisters. Though there would have been other boys of his age in a similar predicament, his childhood was now a thing of the past.

Sometimes salvation comes out of despair. On Wednesday 11 January 1893, William, then aged 15, was sent to the *Exmouth*, a former naval vessel anchored in the Thames estuary off Grays in Essex and used as a training ship for boys preparing to enter the navy.

Even this change may not have been without its trauma for William. It is doubtful that he would have had any choice in the matter or even that it was discussed with him. Though he would be saying goodbye to nearly four years of harsh drudgery in the workhouse, he would also be leaving his mother and his three younger sisters. Perhaps there would have been some solace in the fact that four other boys accompanied him to his new way of life.

HMS *Exmouth* was a former warship of 90 guns, built at Devonport in 1854. In 1877 it was loaned to the Metropolitan Asylums Board as a training ship for boys in a similar situation to William. The boys were drawn from all over the immediate area, normally from the workhouses or from families who had fallen on hard times. The move must have given many boys a window of opportunity to a more positive existence.

The *Exmouth* was manned by navy personnel. The boys slept in hammocks, were taught to wash and mend their clothes, and learnt rowing, sailing and other skills necessary for their future naval careers. They also received a basic education. Every year boys who had finished their training were despatched to the navy proper.

What young William made of his new surroundings is information not available to us. However, there is every indication that he not only accepted his new environment, but strove to make the best of things. In the autumn, he was sent as a boy 2nd class to the *Impregnable*, a naval training ship at Devonport. There followed a succession of training ships, and in 1894 William became a boy 1st class. In 1896, when he was 18, he signed up for a 12-year engagement and was posted to the battleship HMS *Hood*. He was now an ordinary seaman, on the first rung of the ladder of a naval career proper. Twelve months later he was promoted to able seaman. He was again on HMS *Hood*, but there had been several other ships in between, including HMS *Camperdown*, which had featured in one of the worst peacetime naval disasters of all time when on 22 June 1893 it struck HMS *Victoria* during exercises in the Mediterranean, resulting in the sinking of the *Victoria* with the loss of 358 hands.

William worked his way steadily up the ranks, becoming a leading seaman, a petty officer 2nd then 1st class, and finally, in 1917, a chief petty officer. This was a creditable achievement for someone from such a humble background who had clearly made the most of an opportunity.

There is every indication that William kept in touch with his sisters and returned from time to time to his place of birth. On 8 May 1909, then aged 30, he married Louisa Ellen Olivia Daily, aged 29, in St Paul's church, Chatham. One of the witnesses to the wedding was Louisa Hansford, his youngest sister. William and Louisa's first child, William Henry, was born on 18 June 1910, followed on the 30 March 1914 by Nellie Edith Alicia, and on 6 December 1918 by Amy. Sadly, Louisa was a widow when Amy was born. William had been diagnosed with an untreatable stomach cancer the previous year and invalided out of the navy. He died on 8 July 1918. The informant was his sister Louisa.

## Royal Navy ships on which William Edward Hansford served[1]

| 1893 | *Impregnable* | training ship |
|------|---------------|---------------|
| 1893 | *Lion* | training ship |
| 1894 | *Inflexible* | battleship |
| 1895 | *Excellent* | gunboat |
| 1895 | *Australia* | amoured cruiser |
| 1895 | *Grafton* | 1st class cruiser |
| 1895 | *Hood* | battleship |
| 1897 | *Camperdown* | battleship |
| 1897 | *Hood* | battleship |
| 1900 | *Duke of Wellington* | 1st rate |
| 1901 | *Vernon* | torpedo schoolship |
| 1902 | *Victory* | 1st rate |
| 1903 | *Pembroke* | base ship (Chatham) |
| 1903 | *Torch* | sloop |
| 1906 | *Wallaroo* | 2nd class cruiser (harbour service) |
| 1906 | *Wildfire* | base ship (Sheerness) |
| 1906 | *Pegasus* | 6th rate |
| 1907 | *Powerful* | 1st class cruiser |
| 1907 | *Pegasus* | 3rd class cruiser |
| 1909 | *Sappho* | 2nd class cruiser |
| 1909 | *Pembroke* | base ship (Chatham) |

| | | |
|---|---|---|
| 1909 | *Albion* | battleship |
| 1910 | *Newcastle* | 2nd class cruiser |
| 1912 | *Gibraltar* | 1st class cruiser |
| 1913 | *Pembroke* | base ship (Chatham) |
| 1914 | *Euryalus* | armoured cruiser |
| 1916 | *Perth* | armed boarding steamer |
| 1917 | *Euryalus* | armoured cruiser |
| 1918 | *Pembroke* | base ship (Chatham) |

*Note*

1   This is not a complete list. Occasionally William was on two ships in one year. However, it is a good indication of the breadth of his experience.

# THE AUSTRALIAN LINK

The search for Thomas Henry Hansford, my missing great-uncle, took me years. Only recently has new evidence emerged that gives a completely new angle to the question of possible relatives in Australia.

Tracing an ancestor in Australia is not an easy task. To enjoy any degree of success it is necessary to start out with some basic knowledge, such as the name of the ship the person sailed on, the port of departure, or the port of landing in Australia. Without any of this information, the task becomes very much like searching for a needle in a haystack. Research is further complicated by the fact that there are no central records available for Australia in the 19th century: each state maintained its own set. To add to the difficulties, many of the records of arrivals in Australia no longer exist. In fact, it is easier to find a convict than someone who paid for his or her own passage.

There is little doubt that the name Hansford is quite well represented in Australia, including a few individuals with the first names Thomas Henry. However, without managing to locate somebody in Australia who could confirm that one of their ancestors named Thomas Henry Hansford arrived from the UK in the 1870s, I was uncertain whether the one I was searching for did in fact go there.

Despite intensive research and several false trails, it was not until this research document was almost complete that new evidence emerged that finally put success within my reach.

When I started looking into this side of my family history I was faced with a difficult task: where to begin, given the lack of information I possessed. My father's statement 'We think he went to Australia' did not prove that he actually did so. It was certainly insufficient to start any detailed search of Australian records.

Undaunted, I set to, hoping that along the way something might just turn up. I learned that the Guildhall Library held some records of ships leaving the port of London with passengers bound for foreign parts. It seemed a good idea to see what could be gleaned from a visit – Thomas Henry would most likely have departed from London. I set out one rather damp morning and with the aid of my A-Z map managed to find the library without much difficulty. Once I had arrived and gone through bag security I was in the library proper, a huge room filled with individual tables, many of them already occupied with researchers hard at work. There was a very quiet and formal atmosphere. I had to make my enquiry at a desk and order any documents I needed to look at. It was not busy, so I posed my questions to the assistant at the counter. He did his best to be helpful, but he explained that without the name of a ship or more details it was pretty much a hopeless task. He showed me what records they had on the open shelves and I spent a couple of hours looking at them, but beyond being interesting to look at they were of little help in my quest.

I next turned my attention to the Society of Genealogists (SoG). I had joined this organisation early in my research and I knew that their library contained a wealth of family history material. SoG celebrated its centenary in 2011 and now occupies a three-storey building in Goswell Road, London, close to the Barbican. It is not far away from the former Family Records Centre and the London Metropolitan Archives, and through my family history research I now know the area quite well. The SoG building is crammed with material and often I think it looks as if it needs more space for its archives and activities. It has a unique atmosphere of quiet dedication to the task in hand. Conversation is minimal, silence reigns supreme and, unless one asks a question from one of the volunteers manning the enquiry desks, it is possible to speak to no one during an entire visit. I often joke that the SoG is where you will find real family historians.

Before my visit I checked on the SoG website to confirm that there were some Australian records of births, deaths and marriages in the library. I made my way there one bright sunny morning. The SoG membership card opens the security gate, so entry is without any formality. Once inside the building, I made my way to the lower ground floor where all the computers and microfiche readers are housed. I had already discovered that the Australian records I wanted to view were on microfiche. Microfiche is a system of information storage that predates electronic records. The data is recorded on a transparent sheet. Once this is placed on the platen of a microfiche machine it is possible to view the data by moving the platen; it is a fiddly operation, because a small movement of the sheet produces a much larger movement on the screen.

I worked my way through all the available records, looking at each state's records in turn. This entailed several visits and I had to search through a lot of microfiches. I desperately hoped that my research would reveal my elusive ancestor, but sadly I was to be disappointed. I did find a few people named Thomas Henry Hansford, but none of them looked promising. One thing that did impress me during this initial research was the number of Hansfords I discovered. I had read somewhere that Australia was one of the most popular destinations for emigrants in the 19th century, and my findings appeared to confirm this.

I carefully made a note of every Hansford I found, just in case they tied in with any

# THE HANSFORD FAMILY – AUSTRALIAN LINK

Thomas Henry Hansford (1852-1931) arrived in Australia in 1869. After that date all births and deaths shown take place in Australia, unless it is indicated that these take place elsewhere. Marriage locations are listed.

c(circa) = estimated dates, due to non availability of documents.

**FIRST MARRIAGE OF MARY ANN CLARKE**

Mary Ann Clarke
c1846-1906

George Philip Carroll
1837-?
Birth London, England.
m c1864 Melbourne, Australia.

Rebecca Elizabeth
1865-1940

George William
1870-?

---

Thomas Henry Hansford
1830-1903
Birth Chatham, Kent, England.
=
Harriet Eliza Reynolds
c1832-1913
Birth London, England.
m 1850 London, England.

Thomas Henry Hansford
1852-1931
Birth Greenwich, England.

(1) Mary Ann Clarke (Carroll)
c1846-1906
m c1874 Australia or New Zealand.

(2) Annie Sawyer
1879-1959
m 1910 Melbourne, Australia.

Gladys Mary Ann
1910 – 85

Alice Freda
1916-99

Douglas Ernest Peacock
1910-86
m 1940 Melbourne, Australia.

Walter John Stagoll
1914-69
m 1938 Melbourne, Australia.

Mary Ann
c1874-1937

Evangeline
c1877-1951
=
Henry Humphris
1873 -1943
Birth London, England.
m 1894 Melbourne, Australia.

Thomas Patrick
c1877-1962
=
Rose Lillian Rutherford
1878-1958
m 1900 Melbourne, Australia.

Agnes Amelia
c1879-1948

Alfred Wilson
1878-1957
m 1900 Victoria, Australia.

Ellen Maude
c1881-1964

Hilda
1885-86

Bertha Lydia Eileen
c1886-1963
=

Reginald
1890 - 1978

Mabel Newbold
1894 1990
Birth Derbyshire, England.
m 1919 Warminster, England.

Walter 1896-1901
Henry 1897-1945
Evangeline 1899-1965
Ernest 1900-68
Frank 1902-45
Alfred 1906-81
Eric 1908-67
Winifred 1910-88
Edna 1913-2002
Kenneth 1916-?

Doris May 1901-79
Florence Lillian 1903-75
Thomas Henry 1905-78
John William 1907-86
Harold George 1909-73
Ivy Madge 1912-81
Alma Rose 1915-88

Warne 1901-81
Bertha 1903-?
Ila 1906-26
Nellie 1907-27

Dorothy 1921-2010
Reginald 1923-98
Harry 1925-25
William 1926-2005

future research. One in particular caught my attention. This was a birth registered in the state of Victoria for 'Hilda, daughter of Thomas Henry Hansford and Mary Ann Carroll in 1885'. Somehow I felt there might be a link to my family, but it was a slim chance and it needed further investigation.

I continued with other research, but always at the back of my mind was the nagging question of a possible Australian link. On top of that there was the thought that unless I did discover what had happened to my great-uncle, a big gap would remain in my family tree that I would feel bad about – but it was a question of where next to look for clues.

It was my cousin Christine who jerked me back onto the Australian trail. By this time she was also discovering the pleasure of family history research. She knew about my quest for Thomas Henry and one day she contacted me with details of something she had found on the internet. It was an extract from the *St Kilda Times*, the newsletter of the St Kilda Historical Society, and it was a notice from somebody who was seeking information about a Reginald Hansford, born in St Kilda in 1890, the son of Thomas Henry Hansford and Mary Ann née Clarke. St Kilda is a suburb of Melbourne, Australia.

This was interesting. I had already noted a Thomas Henry Hansford in the state of Victoria, but his wife's maiden name was Carroll, not Clarke. Did the two tie up? Why had I not found any record of Reginald Hansford at the SoG? I felt as if I had taken one step forward and two back. Definitely more research was needed.

I found the address and contact details of the secretary of the St Kilda Historical Society on the internet and wrote a letter explaining my mission and enquiring whether there had been any replies to the notice in their journal. I also asked whether the person who had placed the enquiry was a member of the society. Sadly, I had no response, but Christine, who emailed the secretary, received a reply stating that they could not remember the details. As it was three years since the notice had appeared, perhaps this was understandable.

It was a bit of a blow. Once again my hopes were dashed, but that is what family history is like. It was now a case of where to go and what to do next.

It was Christine who again came up with something. She emailed me one day with some details she had found on the Ancestry website. It seemed to be the details of somebody else's research into my ancestor. It listed a Thomas Henry Hansford, born 1852 in Greenwich, Kent, married to a Mary Ann Clarke, born 1846 in Melbourne, and eight children, including a Hilda born in 1885. The entry also gave two death dates: 1936 for Thomas Henry, and 1906 for Mary.

This was intriguing material. For a start, it showed that another researcher had investigated the Thomas Henry Hansford saga, but the most encouraging thing about it for me was that for the first time Greenwich was mentioned, giving a factual link to Australia. It was interesting to observe also that the name Hilda appeared from two different sources. But where had the researcher discovered the rest of the information? It was all so detailed. Now I have always had a tendency to treat with some suspicion material found on websites, often the results of somebody else's research. It is very easy to find someone on the internet and immediately assume he or she is your ancestor. It happens all the time and there is quite a lot of flawed research out there. For me the facts have to be backed up by official documents. However, in this particular case I felt there were grounds for optimism. For the first time I really felt that Thomas Henry had gone to Australia. To be certain, though, I had to have something more concrete.

In the meantime Christine had opened up enquiries on the Ancestry website. Some of the replies she received added to the picture we were building up of Thomas Henry.

One reply confirmed the details we already had, including, among the children born to Thomas Henry and Mary Ann, a son named Reginald. Another reply was more interesting. This suggested that Thomas Henry had been married twice, the second time in 1910 to Annie Sawyer. This information added to the mystery; but with so many different sources all indicating that we were talking about the same Thomas Henry Hansford, it seemed to me that what was required now was some definite proof that he was my ancestor. This could probably only come from Australia.

Because I have ancestors in Kent, I had joined the Kent Family History Society. Curiously, this turned out to be of benefit in my quest for Thomas Henry. The society had a link with Australia, and their journal published details of their contact there. I emailed the lady and she very helpfully suggested that she place an enquiry in her newsletter *Down Under*. Of course I immediately accepted her offer and sent the following details by return:

### CAN ANYBODY HELP?

*I am trying to find out more information on one of my ancestors, Thomas Henry Hansford, who was born in 1852, the eldest son of Thomas Henry and Harriet Eliza Hansford. He was born in Greenwich, London (then part of Kent), but the family later lived in Chatham, Kent. He would have sailed for Australia sometime between the years 1865 and 1875. Unfortunately, I have no details of the ship or port of arrival. If anybody has come across an ancestor who appears to be linked to the above, I would very much appreciate hearing from them.*

The notice appeared in July 2009. I waited expectantly for any replies. My cherished hope was that if Thomas Henry did go to Australia, perhaps there might be a descendant engaged in family history research who might just spot my advert.

It was not to be. I received replies from two very nice people who were clearly anxious to try and help. One more or less confirmed what I already knew. The other was similar, but it stated in addition that Thomas Henry's death was in 1931, not 1936 as indicated in the information posted on the Ancestry site.

So it was more or less back to the drawing board. What was emerging from all the snippets of information so far was that everything appeared to centre on the state of Victoria and in particular the city of Melbourne. This would make further research in Australia easier.

For almost a whole year after this, I did not get much opportunity to do any serious family history research. The little I did manage to do was in other areas, and the Australian link was now bottom of the pile. That did not stop me being aware that this particular side of my family history was still very much unfinished business. When I decided to start writing up all my findings, I felt that I had to have one more attempt to unravel the mystery. If that attempt failed then I would at least feel that I had done everything possible to tie up this last major loose end.

The problem was where to go and what to do. At one stage I even considered trying to locate a professional family history researcher in Australia. However, I rejected that idea on the grounds of expense, as most of the research is carried out on a cost per hour basis, and at the end of it all I might be no further on. I decided to try and get some inside information.

Once again, I contacted the woman who ran the Australian branch of the Kent Family History Society and asked her if she had any ideas for what I might try next. She suggested that I contact a magazine called *Australian Family Tree Connections*, which apparently circulates quite widely in Australia. I decided to follow her advice. It felt like clutching at a straw, but now I was desperate and was happy to explore any avenue open to me. Through the internet I found the details of the magazine, including the email address. I sent off an email to the editor to ask whether the magazine had a 'seeking information' section, explaining why I was making the enquiry. Several weeks passed and I received no reply. I was beginning to think that I was going to have to admit defeat and leave a gap in this side of the story. It was not a palatable decision to have to face, having come so far. Then I heard from the editor of the magazine. She suggested two ways in which they might be able to help: either I could place an advertisement in the magazine, or, if I had an article, she would consider publishing this. I opted for both. I composed an advertisement and wrote a short article entitled 'We think he went to Australia' explaining briefly what I was doing and why, and how much I knew already, and ended with the optimistic thought that I might have distant relatives in Australia who, like me, had an ancestor who had been born in Greenwich.

I sent the article off by email and then waited. I had no idea when it would appear in the magazine. After several weeks I received an email from a woman in Australia who had seen my article and wanted to help. She confirmed that 1931 was the correct death date for Thomas

Henry, quoting details of a death notice from a newspaper dated 30 May 1931. I immediately returned an email expanding the information she would have already read and giving full details of what I knew. Two days later I received a reply. My informant provided me with a list of marriages and deaths she had discovered, all of them related to the list of children I had to hand from the Ancestry website. But the gem of the collection was brief details of Thomas Henry's second marriage. His place of birth was listed as Greenwich England...

It was a thrilling moment. I felt that I had my man. I knew for certain that the birth of no other person called Thomas Henry Hansford had been registered in Greenwich at that time. I just needed to make one more effort to obtain confirmation, and that was close at hand. I took up the offer of my kind helper in Australia to obtain Thomas Henry's second marriage certificate for me.

I will never forget the day that certificate arrived. It compared with the day at Kew all those years ago when I had unearthed so many details about my ancestors in the Greenwich Royal Hospital School records. I felt this time as if I had taken a giant leap in my research. This simple piece of paper showed quite clearly that Thomas Henry Hansford had married Annie Sawyer in the district of Surrey Hills, Victoria on 23 February 1910. It gave his occupation as a gardener and confirmed his father's name as Thomas Henry Hansford, engineer and fitter. Best of all, it quite clearly gave his place of birth as Greenwich, England.

But there was more to come. My contact in Australia also sent me Thomas Henry's death certificate and that of his first wife! Altogether it was a wealth of information. The death certificate confirmed that he had died at Kew (State of Victoria) on 28 May 1931, and it confirmed his place of birth as Greenwich, England. At last a blank space on the family tree had been filled. That precious piece of paper confirmed what my father had said almost 50 years previously. It should be noted that the document contained several anomalies. Thomas Henry's age was given as 76; since he was born in 1852, this should have been 78 or 79. His mother's name appears as Mary Ann (his first wife's name), whereas it should have been Harriet Eliza. Her maiden name is recorded as 'unknown'. However, given the length of time Thomas Henry had been away from England, I feel that these errors are acceptable and do not detract from the value of the document. Ages on certificate do sometimes vary, and it is quite possible that the informant did not know Thomas Henry's mother's name. The information given on both the death certificate and the marriage certificate is consistent.

As so often happens in family history research, as the answer to one question is found, this in turn poses another question. The death certificate of Thomas Henry's first wife, Mary Ann, is a perfect example of this. It shows that she died on 20 February 1906 in Melbourne. It lists all the children of the marriage, and these tie up with those on previous documents. The intriguing piece of information is in the column of marriage details, which shows that her maiden name was Clarke, that at the age of 19 she had married George Carol in Melbourne, and that at the age of 28 she had married Thomas Henry in New Zealand!

That was a real twist to the story. What had my great-uncle been doing in New Zealand? Did he go there straight from England? The questions poured in, but at least now I had a sound basis to work on.

I was quite amazed at the amount of information marriage and death certificates in Australia provide – far in excess of UK ones. From the three documents I had received it was possible to build up a picture of the lives of the people involved. It appeared that in 1864/5*, at the age of 19, Mary Ann Clarke (or Clark), born in Melbourne in 1846*, had married a George Carroll (or Carol), driver. The couple appear to have then gone to New Zealand, but no documentation attesting to this has been discovered. Two children were born: Rebecca in 1865*, and George in 1870*. Both children appear to have been born in Australia. At present I have no information about the fate of George Carroll, but in 1874* Mary Ann married Thomas Henry Hansford. Eight children appear to have been born in this marriage:

Mary Ann (1874-1937)*
Evangeline (1877-1951)*
Thomas Patrick (1877-1962)*
Agnes Amelia (1879-1948)*
Ellen Maude (1881-1964)*
Hilda (1885-1886)*
Bertha Lydia Eileen (1886-1963)*
Reginald (1890-1978)*

The names of the children and their birthdates tie up roughly with the details posted on the Ancestry site. Hilda is the Hilda I had found at the Society of Genealogists. The last child listed must be the Reginald who was mentioned in the St Kilda newsletter.

Four years after Mary Ann died, Thomas Henry married Annie Sawyer.

So there it was. It looked almost certain now that I had found my missing great-uncle. It was now a case of trying to find answers to some of the questions the latest information from Australia had produced. To complete the picture I needed to try and find out where in New Zealand, and when, Thomas Henry had married. In addition, I did not know what had happened to Thomas Henry's two sons, Thomas Patrick and Reginald; they would of course have carried the family name forward if they in turn had married and had children.

---

* The above dates are estimated from the few official documents available. It would appear that most of the births were not registered.

As so often happens in family history research, after a momentous find there followed a period when no progress was made. Now I knew that Thomas Henry Hansford had gone to Australia, but I had not bargained for the sudden appearance of New Zealand as the next area of research to be tackled. The only UK source of any New Zealand records was once again the Society of Genealogists. I spent some time there again hunched over a microfiche reader. I first searched for Thomas Henry's marriage to Mary Ann Carroll and then for the births of any of their children. My efforts came to nought. I found no mention at all of Thomas Henry, and it looked from the records as if there were fewer Hansfords in New Zealand than in Australia. The records I looked at were difficult to read and limited in details, but I felt confident that had there been any information relating to Thomas Henry, I would have spotted it.

The new questions raised by the recent finds were both interesting and intriguing. Had Thomas Henry gone to New Zealand by choice, or had he been a seaman who had jumped ship in a New Zealand port? Was he alone in this enterprise? His cousin John James also disappears from records. Did he or other male members of the family accompany Thomas Henry on his mission? Did that account for my father's belief that more than one family member had disappeared at sea? It is not impossible.

It was now abundantly clear that a new and exciting area of research had opened up. It would take time, more dedication and perhaps a little good fortune to find answers to the questions. One important mystery had been solved: the missing son of Thomas Henry Hansford senior had been found and the gap in the family tree filled, so in that sense the research so far had been effective and successful.

On 24 June 2011 I received an unexpected email containing information beyond my highest expectations. It was again from someone in Australia who had read my article in *Australian Family Tree Connections*. I could hardly believe what I was reading. I had finally made contact with the person who had placed the original enquiry in the St Kilda newsletter. Not only that, but she was a direct descendant of Thomas Henry's son Reginald.

It was a memorable day. I had spent 10 years following up a vague remark. I had pursued many routes that had led nowhere, and had come up against numerous brick walls. Several times I had nearly given up. One final effort had produced a result that I had hardly dreamt could happen. Not only had the mystery of Thomas Henry senior's son been resolved, but I had actually made contact with relatives in Australia.

It was through these newly found relatives that a vital piece of the mystery surrounding Thomas Henry came to light. It has now been established that on 12 February 1869 Thomas Henry Hansford, then aged 16, signed up as a boy member of the crew on the sailing ship *Roxburgh Castle* in London and three days later set sail for Melbourne, Australia. A note is made on the crew list that he had 'not been to sea before'. For his services he was paid 10 shillings per month (50p in today's money). How Thomas Henry fared as a seaman we shall never know. It is possible that he did not like the job, or maybe it was just a step in the direction he wished to take, for on 18 June 1869, three weeks after the *Roxburgh Castle* arrived in Melbourne, Thomas Henry and three other sailors deserted from the ship. The captain, Charles Dinsdale, placed a notice in the *Victoria Police Gazette* of 29 June 1869, offering a reward of £1 each for the arrest of the deserters. In the notice, Thomas Henry is described as being 5 feet 4 inches in height, with dark hair and complexion. From that point on, his life for a while is shrouded in mystery. Certainly to begin with he would have had to keep his whereabouts a secret. Perhaps that is why he does not appear on any records for several years. Some doubt now exists about his marriage in New Zealand, as no further evidence has emerged to link him to that country. It also seems possible that he and Mary Ann were not officially married.

Many questions remain unanswered. Research will continue by me and by my relatives in Australia, who are just as curious as I am to discover more of Thomas Henry's story. Further chapters of this intriguing tale may yet be revealed, but the research so far has answered many questions that 10 years ago were just germinating from vague comments handed down through the generations.

In spite of the difficulties encountered along the way, it has been a fascinating and rewarding journey.

*The Roxburgh Castle*

# THE WORTHINGTON FAMILY

It would be inappropriate to complete a history of the Hansford family without mentioning the link that was made with an old-established Wigan family when my grandfather William Charles Hansford married Mary Worthington in 1885.

As with many surnames, the origins of the name Worthington are somewhat obscure. It is possible that it is derived from a place of the same name, such as Worthington in Leicestershire. It might also come from a family name such as Worth. I have seen suggestions that in this form it dates back to Norman times.

What is apparent is that branches of the Worthington family have lived in Wigan for some considerable time, and most certainly during the period of industrial expansion. Research has shown that the presence of my grandmother's family in the area can be traced back through parish records to the early 18th century.

The earliest Worthington of relevance to this research is Edward, born in Wigan in 1743. I have no details of his marriage, but his son George, born in 1759, married Alice Foster on 2 April 1782. According to the records, she was eight years younger than George. Their son Edward was born in 1794 and married Ann Vose, daughter of Thomas Vose and Mary Jones. It is with the next generation that the records begin to be more informative.

It was when I was researching the life of George Worthington, Edward and Ann's son and my maternal great-grandfather, who was born in 1829, that I encountered one of the oddities in family history that we all come across. On the 2 March 1852, George got married. His bride was Margaret Lawson, who described herself as a spinster. Nothing unusual about that – on the face of it. However, when it came to the birth of their first child, Elizabeth Ann, born on 28 March 1854, Margaret gave her name as Margaret Worthington, formerly Liptrott. She carried out the same procedure with the rest of their children: Thomas, born 30 July 1856, Edward James, born 13 February 1859, Mary, born 29 October 1861, and Annie, born 17 July 1865. So if she was a 24-year-old spinster with the surname Lawson when she got married to George, how did she subsequently become a Liptrott?

When this situation arises, it is very often because there had been a previous marriage, the husband died and the wife reverted to her maiden name. I have come across this several times, and it looked as if something similar might have happened in Margaret's case.

Some investigation into the life of Margaret's mother was required in order to come up with a plausible explanation.

It was largely due to the research carried out by my cousin Christine in Wigan that the picture began to clear and the answers to some of the questions were revealed.

On 23 December 1828, Margaret's mother, Elizabeth Lawson, married Richard Liptrott (or Liptrot). This immediately raises further questions. As Margaret was born on 15 April 1827, was there a previous marriage, or was she born out of wedlock? Research so far has not revealed any definite answers, but the fact that Margaret used two maiden names indicates that she may have been illegitimate. Research on the couple is extremely complex as the records show several Richard Liptrotts and several Elizabeths around the same dates. When looking at the period of time before official records started it is extremely easy to pick up the wrong ancestor.

Richard and Elizabeth went on to have the usual large Victorian family: Alice was born on 25 August 1829, Mary on 6 June 1831, Ann on 5 May 1833, and Elizabeth on 18 September 1835. There are also twins Isabella and Catherine, who were born around 1841.

At the time of the 1841 census, Elizabeth was living in Queen Street, Wigan. She was recorded as head of the household and gave her occupation as 'mangler'. Possibly she was in charge of the public mangle for wringing out excess water from washing. The children listed in the household were Margaret, aged 14, Alice, aged 10, Mary, aged 9, Ann, aged 7, and Elizabeth, aged 5. Only one of the twins, Isabella, aged 6 weeks, is recorded. There is no record of Elizabeth's husband, Richard. It is interesting that this census shows that at the age of 14 Margaret was already working as a reeler, an occupation in the cotton mills.

The next census, ten years later, again shows Elizabeth Liptrott living in Queen Street with all of her family. Once again we have Margaret, aged 23, still a 'reeler', Mary, aged 19, also a reeler, Ann, aged 17, a winder, Elizabeth, aged 15, and Isabella and Catherine, aged 9.

To return to George and Margaret Worthington: after their marriage in All Saints parish church in 1852, it is not until almost 10 years later that we catch up with them again, when the 1861 census records them living at 37 Queen Street. Once again this street turns up in connection with the Worthington family; in fact, over the years many members of the family made their home there – brothers and sisters, sometimes next door to each other. Some of them appear to have been quite adept at running small businesses. Though on the 1861 census George Worthington's occupation appears as 'joiner moulder', ten years later he was running a grocer's shop.

# THE WORTHINGTON AND HANSFORD FAMILY LINK

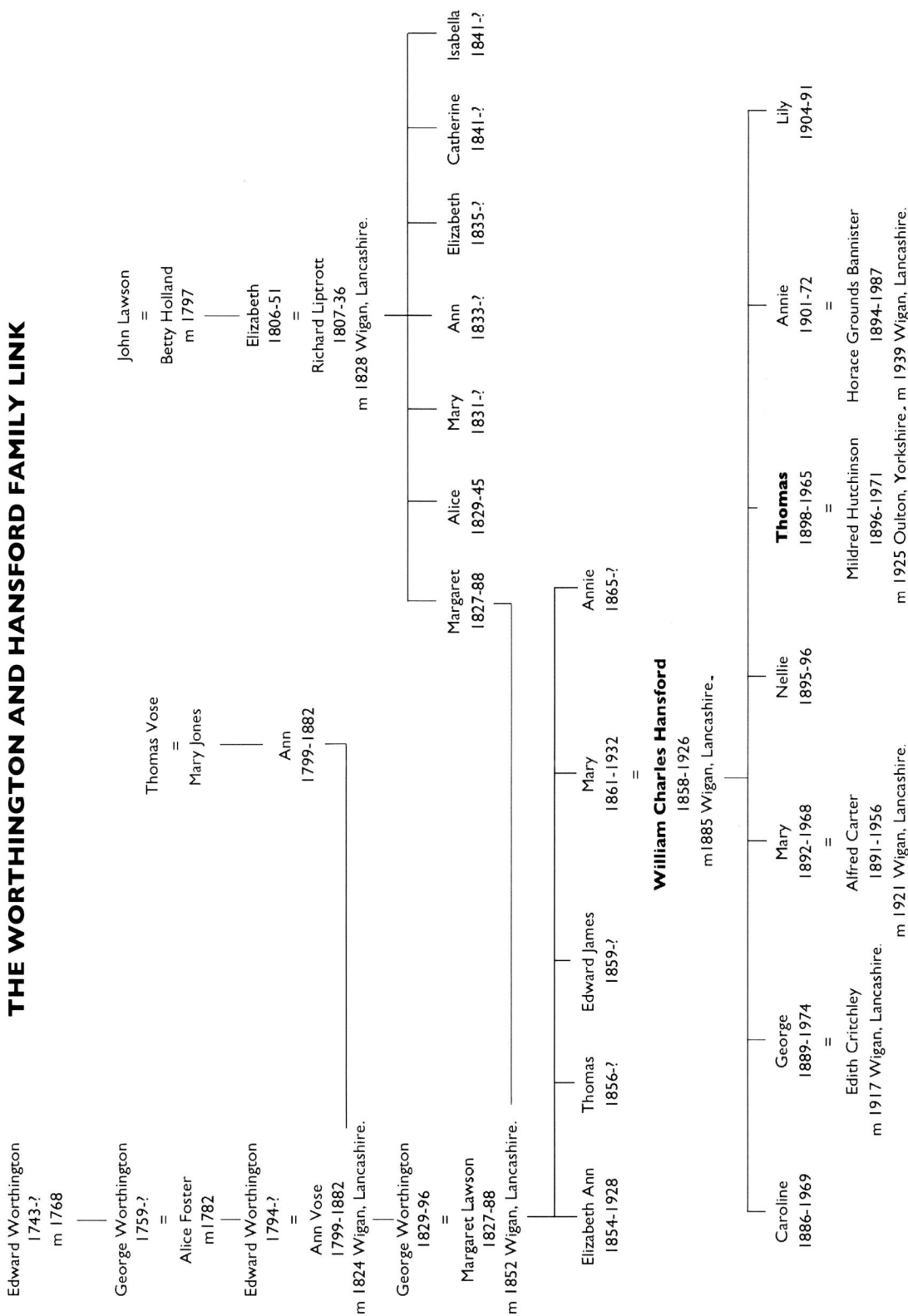

Edward Worthington
1743-?
m 1768

George Worthington
1759-?
=
Alice Foster
m1782

Edward Worthington
1794-?
=
Ann Vose
1799-1882
m 1824 Wigan, Lancashire.

Thomas Vose
=
Mary Jones

Ann
1799-1882

John Lawson
=
Betty Holland
m 1797

Elizabeth
1806-51
=
Richard Liptrott
1807-36
m 1828 Wigan, Lancashire.

George Worthington
1829-96
=
Margaret Lawson
1827-88
m 1852 Wigan, Lancashire.

Margaret
1827-88

Alice
1829-45

Mary
1831-?

Ann
1833-?

Elizabeth
1835-?

Catherine
1841-?

Isabella
1841-?

Elizabeth Ann
1854-1928

Thomas
1856-?

Edward James
1859-?

Mary
1861-1932
=
William Charles Hansford
1858-1926
m1885 Wigan, Lancashire.

Annie
1865-?

Caroline
1886-1969

George
1889-1974
=
Edith Critchley
m 1917 Wigan, Lancashire.

Mary
1892-1968
=
Alfred Carter
1891-1956
m 1921 Wigan, Lancashire.

Nellie
1895-96

Thomas
1898-1965
=
Mildred Hutchinson
1896-1971
m 1925 Oulton, Yorkshire. m 1939 Wigan, Lancashire.

Annie
1901-72
=
Horace Grounds Bannister
1894-1987

Lily
1904-91

The 1861 census also shows that George and Margaret now had three children: Elizabeth, aged 7, Thomas, aged 4, and James, aged 2. What is interesting is that Elizabeth Liptrott's twin daughters, Isabella and Catherine, now aged 19, were living with the family as boarders.

On the 1871 census the family was recorded as still living in Queen Street. George, aged 42, and Margaret, aged 43, were running their grocery shop and now had two more children: my grandmother Mary, aged 9, and Annie, aged just 5. Altogether they appear to have had five children who grew to adulthood.

The situation had changed little by the next census, when George was listed as a 'provision dealer'. He probably ran a small shop built into a house in Queen Street, serving the local population with the basic necessities of life. In those days the average person's diet was simpler than it is today. The housewife's shopping list would have consisted of such items as butter, tea, sugar and bacon, not forgetting essential items such as soap and salt. There would have been a small baker's shop and possibly also a butcher's shop close by. Shopping was very local in those days.

The 1881 census records the last time we find the whole family living together under one roof. George and Margaret's children were all still at home, from the eldest, Elizabeth, then aged 27, to the youngest, Annie, aged 15. All of them by this time would have had paid jobs. Mary, my grandmother, was now aged 19, and it was four years until her marriage to my grandfather.

When looking at these old records on the various census returns, it is tempting to wonder what sort of lives our ancestors lived. The small houses of Queen Street would certainly be considered over-crowded by today's standards. Assuming that George and Margaret turned the front room of their house into a grocery shop, this would have left just the small back room for living accommodation for the whole family. This would have been where the coal-fired cooking range was situated. There would have been a tiny back scullery with a tap and sink, most likely where everybody in the house washed. The toilet would have been in the back yard, or in some cases even at the end of the street. Sleeping accommodation would certainly have denied any personal privacy, and with two or three bedrooms at most, it would have been rather cramped. No doubt George and Margaret would have occupied one room, which they may have shared with a small child or an older daughter. The other bedroom or bedrooms would be used by the rest of the children, with boys in one room and girls in another. It has to be remembered that during this period of history the average family did not have a lot of personal possessions. As regards clothing, the men would have had just their working gear, and a suit kept for Sunday. It was much the same for the girls: one dress for special occasions, perhaps with a pair of boots. It was a long time away from the era of high heels and trainers, and most people would have worn the traditional Lancashire clogs. Robust and with wooden soles, they would have made quite a noise on the cobblestones. A familiar sound to the whole family would have been the early morning 'knocker-up'. This was a person who went around the streets and tapped at windows to rouse the occupants for the day's work in the mills. No need for alarm clocks in those days.

Moving on to the next census, in 1891, things had changed drastically for the family. George Worthington, still a grocer and now aged 62, was a widower, and his daughter Elizabeth, aged 37, the housekeeper. Also living with them was Annie, who listed her occupation as 'confectioner'. So the family were already moving towards a new line of business, which was to feature prominently in the lives of my grandparents in Lorne Street and be continued by my aunts Caroline and Lily right into the 1960s.

The 1901 census shows Elizabeth A. Worthington still living at 37 Queen Street, and now head of the household. She listed her occupation as confectioner and shopkeeper, and with her was her sister Annie, now 35 years old and also a confectioner. The tiny business must have been thriving, because they appear to have employed a servant, Marian Milligen, aged 19 and also a confectioner. Elizabeth would no doubt have been the Auntie Lizzie my father talked about who took him to the Isle of Man for a holiday in the early 1900s. It is quite feasible that much of the expertise in confectionery knowledge displayed in the shop at Lorne Street originated with Elizabeth. It seems that she was also well skilled in other culinary arts. My father once told me a story about her when we were passing through the small Cheshire town of Northwich. He glanced towards the solid Victorian hotel dominating the square and remarked. 'My Auntie Lizzie once had a job there as cook.' The rest of the story was rather intriguing. It appeared that on the first day of her employment, after a hard morning preparing lunch, Elizabeth asked the waitress to fetch her a glass of stout from the bar. The landlord took a dim view of this request and as a result Elizabeth walked out, clearly confident that she had the skill and the reputation to find another job quickly.

The Worthington family's link with the Hansfords was a close one, and their deep association with Wigan would be well worth further research.

# THE HUTCHINSON FAMILY

When I started my family history research, I knew more about my mother's side of the family than my father's. However, this was mainly in the form of little snippets of information. For example, I knew that my mother had been born in Yorkshire, in a place called Oulton, near Rothwell and not far from the city of Leeds. I knew that she was the youngest of the family and that she had brothers and sisters; one of these, her older sister Beatrice, my Auntie Beatty, I knew reasonably well, because she paid us visits. I knew that my mother's parents had both worked at Oulton Hall, a minor stately home, my grandfather as a gardener and my grandmother as housekeeper. My mother had also told me that she had spent part of her childhood living with an aunt in Bristol.

These few basic bits of information were enlivened by the comments my mother would make from time to time, such as, 'Your uncle Willy fought in the First World War,' or 'It took your grandmother an hour to go round Oulton Hall and open or shut all the windows.' She also recalled that, as the owners of the hall travelled the world a good deal and left the hall in the safe keeping of her parents, she and her brothers and sisters had a great time playing there. All these remarks, while interesting at the time, were of little practical use to a small boy who at that period had never even heard of family history.

It was not until I had been researching my family history for several years that I started to look at my mother's side of the family, the Hutchinsons. By this time I had traced the Hansford line back several generations and along the way had found out a good deal about the Worthingtons, my grandmother's family on my father's side; but my knowledge of my mother's ancestry remained extremely sparse. I dabbled into it from time to time but did not make a great deal of progress. One thing I did find out was that the surname Hutchinson was very common in Yorkshire. I managed to obtain my grandparents' marriage certificate, which proved to be a good starting point. This document showed that they were married in St John's church, Oulton on 19 May 1888. My grandfather's father's name appeared as Thomas Barber, occupation gardener. This was puzzling. My grandmother's father's name was recorded as Mark Woodruffe, miner. A good start, but the details clearly raised a few questions.

It was not until the 1901 census was released that I made significant progress. This showed my Hutchinson grandparents and their children living in 172 Leeds Road, Oulton, in the West Riding of Yorkshire: my grandfather William, my grandmother Lucy, my aunts and uncles Beatrice, aged 12, William, aged 10, Elizabeth, aged 8, Henry, aged 6, and lastly my mother, Mildred, aged 4. All had been born in Oulton except my grandmother, who gave her place of birth as Winterbourne, Gloucestershire.

With the aid of this information, I was able eventually to obtain the birth certificates for most of my aunts and uncles, though I did have difficulty sometimes locating the correct person in those large books at the Family Records Centre. There seemed to be so many people named William or Henry Hutchinson.

Next I turned my attention to the 1891 census. William Hutchinson, aged 30, a gardener, was comparatively easy to find, together with his wife, Lucy Maria, also aged 30. This time she gave her place of birth as Bristol, but I had already discovered that Winterbourne was close to that city. Also listed on the census form were Beatrice, aged 2, and 2-month-old

*William Hutchinson c1860-1927*

William. However, the most valuable piece of information for me was that Emma Hutchinson, my grandfather's mother, was shown as living with the family.

So now I had the name of one of my great-grandmothers on my mother's side. The next step was to look at the transcript of the 1881 census. This showed William and his mother living at the Three Horse Shoes Inn, Oulton. No other members of the family were present. This was interesting but my search did not reveal any new information about the other family members.

It was necessary to go back another ten years to the 1871 census to find out more. What this search revealed was more intriguing. The Oulton return showed Ann Hutchinson, aged 75, as head of the household. She described herself as an annuitant, so it looked as if she was receiving an income from somewhere. Living with her were her two daughters Emma and Mary, and three grandchildren John, aged 22, Mary, aged 11, and William, also aged 11, who must have been my grandfather. So it looked as if I had come across my great-great-grandmother. It was not possible at this stage to identify who was the son or daughter of whom except for William. The family's address was recorded as 'Grocers Shop'. Interestingly, there were no husbands listed on the census return for either 1871 or 1881. When this situation presents itself in family history, it often means one of two things: either we are dealing with a single woman and an illegitimate child, or her husband has died. To find out more I would have to go back still further.

These days it is hard to imagine doing family history research without access to a computer and the internet, which despite its shortcomings is extremely useful for checking such things as the census records, albeit often for a fee. It was not too difficult, then, for me to access the 1861 census and do a check on Ann Hutchinson, then aged 66, and her family. The return again shows her living at the Three Horse Shoes. No occupation is listed for her. With her were my great-grandmother Emma, aged 36, and Emma's children James, aged 12, Mary Emma, aged 1 month, and my grandfather William, aged 1. Unfortunately, the information gleaned from this census raised further questions and did not answer the previous ones. For example, what was Ann Hutchinson doing living in a public house? Was she the landlady, or was she married to the landlord? In the latter case it seems a bit odd for her daughter and grandchildren to have been living with her. To try and locate answers, only two courses of action were open to me: to go back further on the census, or to look at the records for St John's church, Oulton. As the records for the parish in question were not available to me online, I opted to continue with the census for the time being.

On the 1851 census, again the family is at the Three Horse Shoes. Ann, aged 56, was head of the household, but is listed as a pauper. Also in the household were daughter Emma, aged 26, and this time a son, John, aged 24, a stonemason. One grandson appears on the return: John, aged 2.

This was a bit more information, but yet again the results produced more questions than answers. Why was Ann Hutchinson listed as a pauper, and how did the Three Horse Shoes Inn come into the picture? Sometimes in cases like this it pays to look at the original pages of the census; the information I had gleaned so far had come from transcripts. Fortunately, I had access to the entire census through my computer.

A look at the original pages did partly answer some of the questions. On the 1871 census there was no indication that Ann Hutchinson and her two daughters were keeping a shop. In fact, Emma and Mary both gave their occupation as 'charwoman'. Though parts of the page were difficult to read, it did appear that Ann was a widow.

The 1851 census was interesting because this is where according to the transcript Ann is described as a pauper. What is striking is that the original entry has been crossed out and replaced by the word 'pauper'. Owing to the poor quality I could not make out what the original word was. As no male partners are listed on these returns it looks as if Ann Hutchinson was a widow and Emma and Mary were unmarried, but to date I have not been able to substantiate this.

I had hoped that the 1841 census might provide a clue to Ann's husband or partner, but I found it extremely difficult to pick the family up on this census.

*Lucy Maria Hutchinson 1860-1942*

The most logical next step to take would be to make a visit to Leeds and look at the records for St John's church, Oulton to see if they reveal any additional information.

Since delving into the history of this side of the family, I have wondered how my maternal grandparents met. On the 1881 census, my grandmother Lucy, aged 20, was working as a parlour maid to a Mrs Cecilia Mostyn, the widow of an army surgeon. It appears to have been quite an affluent household, because in addition a cook and a gardener were employed. The residence was at Downend, which is north-west of Bristol. All the details relating to Lucy's early life mention villages in this area.

The next available record for Lucy was in 1888, when she married my grandfather. This time she stated that her residence at the time of her marriage was Oulton. How did she come to move from Bristol to Oulton? We shall probably never find out, but one suggestion is that it was through her employment. These wealthy families often knew each other, and good servants were hard to come by. There is no evidence to support this theory in the case of Lucy, but it is quite feasible. It is also not inconceivable that it was through working at Oulton Hall that my grandmother met my grandfather, who worked in the gardens there.

Information about Lucy's early life and background has largely been gleaned from the various censuses. At the time of the 1871 census the family were living at Rain Hill, Westerleigh, another village in Gloucestershire not far from Bristol. The head of the household was Mark Woodruffe, aged 36, a miner. His wife, Maria, was the same age. The other people registered in the household that night consisted of their eldest daughter, Elizabeth, aged 13, my grandmother Lucy Maria, aged 10, Beatrice Louise, aged 8, and Sarah Ann, just 1 month old. It is interesting that on the various census returns, the family name has several different spellings. I have encountered 'Woodruffe' and even 'Woodriff'.

I have obtained the marriage certificate for my maternal great-grandparents Mark and Maria. The ceremony took place in the parish church of Mangotsfield on 14 March 1857. Both were aged 22 and were residents of Mangotsfield. Mark gave his occupation as 'collier'. One particularly useful piece of information obtained from this document is that Maria's maiden name was Andrews. Her father was Isaac Andrews, a gardener.

I did a little research into the Andrews family. Isaac Andrews is listed as an agricultural labourer on several of the census returns. He appears to have been born around 1809, and Elizabeth, his wife, five years later. The 1841 census also lists Henry, aged 11, and Maria, aged 5. It appears, then, that both Isaac and Elizabeth were born in the county of Gloucestershire and spent their lives in villages to the north-west of Bristol.

I have yet to discover which of her aunts my mother stayed with in Bristol during her

# THE HUTCHINSON AND HANSFORD FAMILY LINK

Charles Woodruffe
=
Hannah ?

Isaac Andrews
c1809-?
=
Elizabeth
c1813-?

Ann Hutchinson
c1795-?

Henry
c1830-?

Maria
c1835-?

Charles
c1844-?

William
c1846-?

Emma
c1825-?

William
c1827-?

Mary
c1834-?

Mark Woodruffe
c1835-?
=
Maria Andrews
c1835-?
m 1857 Mangotsfield, Gloucestershire.

Lucy Maria
1860-1942

Beatrice Louis
c1863-?

Sarah Ann
1865-?

William Hutchinson
c1860-1927
=
Lucy Maria Woodruffe
1860-1942
m 1888 Oulton, Yorkshire.

Elizabeth M.F.
c1858-?

Beatrice
1888-?

William
c1891-?

Elizabeth
c1893-?

Henry
c1894-?

**Mildred**
1896-1971
=
**Thomas Hansford**
1898-1965
m 1925 Oulton, Yorkshire.

childhood. On the 1901 census her grandmother Maria, aged 66, was living at Winterbourne Down. With her were her daughters Beatrice, aged 38, and Sarah Ann, aged 30. Maria and Beatrice are described as tailoresses. There is no mention of Elizabeth, Maria's eldest daughter, but a granddaughter of Maria's, Violet Parfitt, aged 11, appears in the household on the census, so it seems likely that Elizabeth was married.

Clearly a great deal more research would be needed to tie up all the loose ends on this side of the family.

# PART 3

# ORIGINS OF THE NAME HANSFORD

When looking at the background of a surname, one important fact that soon becomes clear is that the use of surnames is a comparatively recent innovation.

In earlier times it was mainly the aristocracy that had family names; the poorer people often adopted names associated with their trade or with the place they came from. Some of these have come down through history and are with us today. Names derived from a trade are often easily identifiable, such as Baker, Butcher and Carpenter. Names taken from places include Hamilton and Burton. Some names were originally descriptive of personal appearance: examples are Whitehead and Long. Even place names linked to geographical features make an appearance. Hill and Wood are examples.

As is often the case, it was the administration or government of the day that initiated the changes required for certain parts of the population to be identifiable. Many historians consider the compiling of the Domesday Book of 1086 to be one of the first attempts in English history to do this. This led to the gradual adoption of surnames, particularly by the aristocracy, during the 13th and 14th centuries. However, it was the introduction of poll or personal taxation that generated the need for every citizen to have a surname. By the beginning of the 15th century most English families had hereditary surnames, although it was not until the 19th century that spellings began to be standardised.

It is against this background that we look at the origins of the family name Hansford. It is surprising how little research appears to have been done into the name until recently. In the early days of my research, I spent a little time in a well-stocked library, glancing through the books of surnames. I was amazed to find that in the half-dozen or so volumes I looked at there was no mention of the name Hansford. However, the popularity of family history research has changed this, and a number of publications now list their findings for the name. In addition, there is a mass of information on the internet.

Given that its roots are not readily identifiable, it is not surprising that several different theories exist on the origins of the name Hansford. The most popular is that it is a place name, but identifying the actual place is not so easy. Most historians think it is highly likely to be Ansford in Somerset, a place listed in the Domesday Book as Almundesford and derived from the Old English personal name Ealhmund plus *ford*, meaning a place by the river or 'river crossing'.

However, there is another group of historians who believe that the name has connections with other places in England, such as Handforth in Cheshire or Hanford in Dorset and Staffordshire, though it could be argued that these locations would only spawn the names Handforth and Hanford.

A third group of people believe that the name had deeper Saxon roots. Hans is a name readily recognised in modern Germany and is quite likely an abbreviation of the Christian name Johannes. I have observed that in Germany nobody seems to have any problem spelling my name, unlike in the UK where it is often spelt incorrectly as 'Hanford' or 'Handsford'. The Old English word *ford* does of course feature in many of our present-day place names, such as Oxford, Hertford and Bedford.

With these three almost conflicting opinions, I set out to try and sift through the evidence. The ten-yearly census that has been carried out from the year 1841 provides a good guide to the distribution of the name throughout England. From these records it becomes clear that the name has its roots firmly in South West England, with Dorset leading the way on every occasion. In 1841 Dorset had almost four times the number of Hansfords as its nearest rival, Somerset. London is next and Devon a rather poor fourth. There is a tendency for this pattern to continue throughout the history of census-taking. What is also apparent is the spread of the name to the rest of the country during the 19th century, with counties with a seaboard such as Kent and Hampshire doing better than the landlocked ones, no doubt due to seafaring Hansfords.

While I accept that derivation from the place name Ansford is the most popular explanation, I have not been entirely happy with the adding of an 'H' to the name. In my experience it is more usual to find a letter dropped. I have encountered this several times in my family history research. One of James Hansford senior's sons was incorrectly named Ansford in the parish register. When James wanted to get this particular son into Greenwich Royal Hospital School and needed to produce a marriage certificate to support his application, the family had to write to the parson and obtain an affidavit confirming that a mistake had been made.

Going by the facts available from the census records, it is surprising that Somerset is not the leading county for concentration of the name Hansford. As records show, it lags well behind Dorset. It is possible that we are dealing here with early migration from one county to another, though a mass migration seems a bit odd. During the 17th and 18th centuries the

West Country was largely rural and a high proportion of the population would have earnt a living on the land, as many records show. It does not seem feasible that large numbers of these people would have moved about a great deal. With all the counties involved having a coastline, it was only natural that some members of the community would have drifted off to sea and spread roots that way. My own family history is proof of this.

It is always pleasant and rewarding in research to find definite answers. Researching surnames is wide open to speculation, because there is often insuffient evidence to confirm or refute the various theories that have been generated over time regarding their origins.

I am of the opinion that the suggestion that my own family name originates in Cheshire or Staffordshire can be dismissed entirely, though as has already been suggested this theory may account for variations such as Handforth. Regarding the theory that the name springs from Ansford in Somerset, I accept that the idea is feasible, but this does not explain the high number of Hansfords in the adjoining county of Dorset. My belief is that there are some deeper Saxon connections, but there is no way of proving this.

In conclusion, what is apparent is that the history of the name Hansford is deeply embedded in the history of England, and that it is a very old name – older than the family names linked to the Norman invasion of 1066. This fact alone makes any conclusive research almost impossible, and rather sadly we are left with a lot of speculation.

# NOTABLE DATES – HISTORICAL, GENEALOGICAL AND FAMILY

| 1066 | Battle of Hastings |
|------|--------------------|
| 1086 | Domesday Book |
| 1509 | Henry VIII ascends the throne |
| 1538 | Parish registration compulsory in the UK |
| 1558 | Elizabeth I on throne |
| 1588 | Spanish Armada |
| 1598 | Bishops' Transcripts initiated |
| 1625 | Charles I ascends the throne |
| 1649-60 | Commonwealth (Interregnum) |
| 1660 | Restoration |
| | Charles II ascends the throne |
| 1662 | Poor Relief Act |
| 1681 | Royal Hospital Chelsea founded |
| 1685 | James II ascends the throne |
| 1689 | William and Mary ascend the throne |
| 1694 | Greenwich Hospital founded |
| 1702 | Anne ascends the throne |
| 1714 | George I ascends the throne |
| 1727 | George II ascends the throne |
| 1733 | All legal documents to be written in English |
| 1749 | Navy List first published |
| 1752 | Change from the Julian to the Gregorian calendar |
| 1760 | George III ascends the throne |
| 1761 | Start of regimental registers for armed forces births, marriages and deaths |
| **1770** | **James Hansford senior born in Swyre, Dorset** |

| | |
|---|---|
| 1775-83 | American War of Independence |
| 1785 | First issue of *The Times* |
| **1788** | **First record of James Hansford senior on a naval ship** |
| | First Fleet arrives in Australia |
| 1789 | French Revolution |
| 1791 | Ordnance Survey established |
| 1803-1815 | Napoleonic Wars |
| **1796** | **James Hansford senior marries Elizabeth Colliver in Fowey, Cornwall** |
| | Death duties introduced |
| 1789 | George Washington becomes US President |
| **1801** | **James Hansford senior appointed a warrant officer** |
| 1801 | First census |
| **1802** | **James Hansford junior born in Fowey, Cornwall** |
| 1805 | Battle of Trafalgar |
| 1804 | First railway steam locomotive journey |
| 1815 | Battle of Waterloo |
| 1819 | Peterloo Massacre |
| 1820 | George IV ascends the throne |
| **1824** | **James Hansford junior marries Eliza Spencelayh in Frindsbury, Kent** |
| 1828 | The Duke of Wellington becomes prime minister |
| 1829 | Metropolitan Police founded |
| **1830** | **Thomas Henry Hansford born in Chatham, Kent** |
| | William IV ascends the throne |
| | Liverpool & Manchester Railway opened |
| 1831 | Cholera epidemic in England |
| **1833** | **James Hansford junior dies aged 30 of cholera in Chatham, Kent** |
| 1834 | Tolpuddle Martyrs arrested |
| 1837 | Queen Victoria ascends the throne |
| | Civil registration introduced in England and Wales |
| **1838** | **Eliza Hansford (Spencelayh) dies aged 32 in Chatham, Kent** |
| | Public Record Office established |
| **1840** | **Elizabeth Hansford (Colliver) dies aged 68 in Chatham, Kent** |
| | Postage stamps introduced |
| 1841 | First UK census for which searchable records exist |

| | |
|---|---|
| **1841-5** | **Thomas Henry Hansford at Greenwich Hospital School** |
| **1845** | **James Hansford (senior) dies aged 79 in Chatham, Kent** |
| 1845-52 | The Great Famine (Ireland) |
| 1846 | Corn Laws repealed |
| **1850** | **Thomas Henry Hansford marries Harriet Eliza Reynolds in Waterloo, London** |
| 1851 | UK census |
| | **Thomas Henry and Harriet Eliza Hansford recorded in Greenwich, Kent** |
| | Great Exhibition |
| 1853 | Royal Navy introduces continuous service engagement book |
| 1853-6 | Crimean War |
| 1855 | Civil registration introduced in Scotland |
| 1856 | Victoria Cross first awarded |
| 1857 | Indian Mutiny |
| | Civil divorce introduced |
| **1858** | **William Charles Hansford born in Chatham, Kent** |
| | Central probate system introduced |
| 1861 | UK census |
| | **Thomas Henry Hansford and family recorded in Chatham, Kent** |
| | Start of American Civil War |
| 1864 | Introduction of civil registration in Ireland |
| 1866 | Age of the deceased shown on death certificates |
| 1870 | Establishment of universal education |
| 1871 | UK census |
| | **Thomas Henry Hansford and family recorded in Loose, nr Maidstone, Kent** |
| 1875 | Penalties introduced for failure to register births, marriages and deaths |
| 1879 | Anglo-Zulu War |
| 1881 | UK census |
| | **Thomas Henry Hansford and family recorded in Wigan, Lancs.** |
| 1882 | Married Women's Property Act |
| **1885** | **William Charles Hansford marries Mary Worthington in Wigan, Lancs.** |
| 1887 | Queen Victoria's Golden Jubilee |
| 1891 | UK census |

|  | **Thomas Henry Hansford and family recorded in Wigan, Lancs.** |
|---|---|
| 1897 | Queen Victoria's Diamond Jubilee |
| **1898** | **Thomas Hansford born in Wigan, Lancs** |
| 1899-1902 | Boer War |
| 1901 | UK census |
|  | **Thomas Henry Hansford and family recorded in Wigan, Lancs.** |
|  | Edward VII ascends the throne |
| **1903** | **Thomas Henry Hansford dies aged 73 in Wigan, Lancs.** |
|  | First powered flight of the Wright brothers |
| 1909 | First aeroplane flight across the English Channel by Louis Blériot |
| 1910 | George V ascends the throne |
| 1911 | Society of Genealogists founded |
|  | UK census |
|  | Mother's maiden name first shown in GRO birth indexes |
| 1912 | Names of both husband and wife first shown in GRO marriage indexes |
|  | Sinking of the *Titanic* |
| **1913** | **Harriet Eliza Hansford (Reynolds) dies aged 81 in Wigan, Lancs.** |
| 1914-18 | First World War |
| 1916 | Conscription introduced |
| 1918 | Royal Air Force founded |
|  | Women's suffrage granted |
| 1919 | First direct non-stop transatlantic flight by Alcock and Brown |
| 1921 | Ireland divided into Irish Free State and Northern Ireland |
| **1925** | **Thomas Hansford marries Mildred Hutchinson in Oulton, Yorks.** |
| **1926** | **William Charles Hansford dies aged 67 in Wigan, Lancs.** |
| **1927** | **Kenneth Leslie Hansford born in Oulton, Yorks.** |
|  | Adoption introduced as a legal process |
| 1929 | Poor Law amended. Workhouses abolished |
| **1932** | **Mary Hansford (Worthington) dies aged 70 in Wigan, Lancs.** |
| **1935** | **Beverley (Gordon) Hansford born in Dartington, Devon** |
| 1936 | Edward VIII ascends the throne |
|  | Abdication crisis |
|  | George VI ascends the throne |
| 1939 | Identity cards introduced |
| 1939-45 | Second World War |
| 1940 | Battle of Britain |

| | |
|---|---|
| 1946 | National Insurance Act heralds the welfare state |
| 1951 | Festival of Britain |
| 1952 | Elizabeth II ascends the throne |
| 1956 | Suez Crisis |
| 1961 | Institute of Heraldic and Genealogical Studies founded |
| **1965** | **Thomas Hansford dies age 67 in Winsford, Cheshire** |
| **1970** | GRO records moved from Somerset House to St Catherine's House |
| **1971** | **Mildred Hansford (Hutchinson) dies aged 75 in Leeds, Yorks.** |
| | Decimalisation of UK currency system |
| 1974 | Federation of Family History Societies founded |
| 1977 | Public Record Office at Kew opens |
| 1997 | Family Records Centre opens |
| 2008 | Family Records Centre closes |

# DOCUMENTARY SOURCES

It would be impossible to list in detail all the documents consulted. The following are the more important documents that contain information relevant to this family history research.

## GENERAL REGISTER OF BIRTHS, MARRIAGES AND DEATHS

Indexes and certificates from 1837 on

## THE NATIONAL CENSUS

1841, 1851, 1861, 1871, 1881, 1891, 1901, 1911

## LOCAL RECORDS

### London Metropolitan Archives

St Alfege, Greenwich

| Baptisms | 1821-1830 | X094/112 |
|----------|-----------|----------|
|          | 1830-1834 | X094/113 |
|          | 1849-1853 | X094/114 |

St John the Evangelist, Waterloo Road, London

| Marriages | 1843-1846 | X092/105 |
|-----------|-----------|----------|
|           | 1849-1852 | X092/107 |

St Nicholas, Deptford Green

| Marriages | 1813-1937 | X097/251 |

## Medway Archives And Local Studies Centre

All Saints, Frindsbury, Kent

| Marriages | 1822-1830 | 00000250 (1824) |
| | 1822-1830 | 00000252 (1824) |
| | 1831-1837 | 00000387 (1835) |

St Margaret of Antioch, Rochester, Kent

| Baptisms | 1783-1812 | 00000046 (1806) |

| Marriages | 1819-1937 | 00000076 (1828) |
| | 1819-1937 | 00000092 (1829) |

St Mary the Virgin, Chatham, Kent

| Baptisms | 1813-1816 | MF 483 00020357 (1814) |
| | 1816-1820 | MF 483 00020559 (1819) |
| | 1823-1826 | MF 484 00030147 (1826) |
| | 1826-1830 | MF 484 00030220 (1828) |
| | 1830-1834 | MF 484 00030312 (1830) |
| | 1830-1834 | MF 484 00030322 (1830) |
| | 1830-1834 | MF 484 00030413 (1832) |

| Marriages | 1837-1841 | MF 489 00080425 (1839) |

| Burials | 1813-1817 | MF 494 00130006 (1813) |
| | 1833-1837 | MF 494 00130622 (1833) |
| | 1828-1833 | MF 494 00130486 (1829) |
| | 1837-1843 | MF 495 00140042 (1838) |

| 1837-1843 | MF 495 00140051 (1839) |
| 1837-1843 | MF 495 00140118 (1840) |
| 1843-1846 | MF 495 00140291 (1845) |
| 1856-1863 | MF 495 00140689 (1858) |
| 1868-1872 | MF 496 00150245 (1869) |
| 1875-1877 | MF 496 00150383 (1875) |
| 1875-1877 | MF 496 00150400 (1876) |

## Wigan History Shop (Museum of Wigan Life)

St Thomas, Wigan

| Baptisms | MF 1A 35/1 | No. 407 | George Hansford |
| | | No. 750 | Mary Hansford |
| | | No. 1177 | Thomas Hansford |
| | | No. 1470 | Annie Hansford |
| | | No. 1668 | Lily Hansford |

Wigan Borough Cemetery, Lower Ince, Wigan

Burials    MF4B/17

## THE NATIONAL ARCHIVES

During the course of research, over 150 naval documents were viewed at The National Archives. Listed below are those of greatest relevance to the Hansford family.

| PIECE NO. | TITLE AND DATE RANGE (SPECIFIC DATES IN PARENTHESES) | RELATING TO |
| --- | --- | --- |
| ADM6/191 | Warrant issue and fee book: pursers, gunners, boatswains and carpenters 1800-1815 | James Hansford Snr |
| ADM6/303 | Register of applicants to Greenwich Hospital for admission, out-pensions or other relief (1842) | Thomas Reynolds |

| ADM11/31 | Succession book of standing officers 1812-1817 | James Hansford Snr |
|---|---|---|
| ADM11/36 | Survey of boatswains' services 1816-1818 | James Hansford Snr |
| ADM22/52 | Pensions paid at Chatham 1831-1837 | James Hansford Snr |
| ADM29/19 | Greenwich: warrant officers and ratings Jan. 1838-Feb. 1840 | James Hansford Jnr |
| ADM29/98 | Service records 1802-1868 E-L | Hansford |
| ADM35/124 | Pay book *Abundance* Oct. 1799-Mar. 1805 | James Hansford Snr |
| ADM35/955 | Pay book *Leviathan* Oct. 1790-Sep. 1793 | James Hansford Snr |
| ADM35/1604 | Pay book *Sans Pareil* Nov. 1795-Apr. 1796 | James Hansford Snr |
| ADM35/1611 | Pay book *Saint George* Oct. 1787- Dec. 1790 | James Hansford Snr |
| ADM35/1612 | Pay book *Saint George* Mar. 1791 – Sep. 1791 | James Hansford Snr |
| ADM35/1623 | Pay book *Sprightly* Jul. 1785 – Dec. 1788 | James Hansford Snr |
| ADM35/3172 | Pay book *Thames* Jul. 1806 – Apr. 1809 | James Hansford Snr |
| ADM35/4056 | Pay book *Blossom* Jul. 1817 – Jun. 1824 | James Hansford Jnr |
| ADM35/4551 | Pay book *Prince Regent* Aug. 1830 – Feb. 1832 | James Hansford Jnr |
| ADM35/2587 | Pay book *Armide* Aug. 1809 – Dec. 1811 | James Hansford Snr |
| ADM36/10882 | Muster book *Sprightly* Jul. 1787 – Nov. 1791 | James Hansford Snr |
| ADM36/11177 | Muster book *Childers* Nov. 1789 – Oct. 1791 | James Hansford Snr |
| ADM36/11662 | Muster book *Sans Pareil* Mar. 1795 – Mar. 1797 | James Hansford Snr |
| ADM36/11739 | Muster book *Leviathan* Feb. 1793 – Apr. 1794 | James Hansford Snr |
| ADM37/2488 | Muster book *Armide* Sep. 1810 – Apr. 1811 | James Hansford Snr |
| ADM37/8223 | Muster book *Ocean* Nov. 1831-Aug. 1833 | James Hansford Jnr |
| ADM45/19 | Navy Board, and Admiralty, Accountant General's Department: officers' and civilians' effects papers (1845) | James Hansford Snr |
| ADM73/46 | General register of pensioners and their families 1833-1846 | Thomas Reynolds |
| ADM73/48 | General register of pensioners and their families 1846-1863 | Thomas Reynolds |
| ADM73/60 | Rough entry book of pensioners 1839-1846 | Thomas Reynolds |
| ADM73/411 | Greenwich Hospital School admission of boys 1821-1865 | Thomas H. Hansford William Hansford |
| ADM73/247 | Greenwich Hospital School admission papers Hams-Hare 1726-1870 | Caroline Hansford James Hansford Jnr Samuel Hansford Thomas H. Hansford William Hansford |
| ADM139/92 | Royal Navy continuous service engagement book | Samuel Hansford |

| ADM171/61 | Miscellaneous medal roll 1866-1966 | William E. Hansford |
| ADM171/75 | Index to medal rolls 1914-1918 | William E. Hansford |

## NATIONAL NEWSPAPER LIBRARY

*NEWS OF THE WORLD*

5 March 1939
2 April 1939
16 April 1939

# ACKNOWLEDGEMENTS

Many people have contributed to the completeness of this research and I would like to take this opportunity of expressing my thanks to them all. I am particularly indebted to the following:

MICHAEL HANSFORD, for suggestions during research and information on Dorset ancestors.

CHRISTINE ROSS, for valuable research carried out into the Wigan side of the family.

HELEN TRACEY, for clarifying the original Australian information.

JILL & KEVIN KELWIG, for help and support detailing the family link to Australia.

HELEN BANKS, for proofreading and editing.

CASEMATE PUBLISHERS and FRONTLINE BOOKS, for permission to use information from *Ships of the Royal Navy: The Complete Record of All Fighting Ships of the Royal Navy from the 15th Century to the Present* by J.J. Colledge, revised and updated by Ben Warlow (2010).

THE NATIONAL ARCHIVES, for permission to reproduce information from the ADM series of records.

NATIONAL MARITIME MUSEUM, for permission to use the pictures of the Roxburgh Castle and the boy from Greenwich Royal Hospital School.

ST. JOHN THE EVANGELIST CHURCH, WATERLOO, for permission to use the 1880 illustration of the church.

*Acknowledgements*

MEDWAY ARCHIVES, for permission to use the images of Chatham.

MAGGIE WOODRUFF, Australian agent, Kent Family History Society, for pointing me in the right direction with the Australian branch of the family.

LLOYDS REGISTER GROUP SERVICES LTD, for assistance in tracing further details on the sailing ship Roxburgh Castle.

# BIBLIOGRAPHY

| | |
|---|---|
| Aspin, Chris | *The Cotton Industry* (2000) |
| Christian, Peter | *The Genealogist's Internet* (2002) |
| Colledge, J.J. | *Ships of the Royal Navy: The Complete Record of All Fighting Ships of the Royal Navy from the 15th Century to the Present*, revised and updated by Ben  Warlow (2010) |
| Fletcher, Mike | *The Making of Wigan* (2005) |
| Grundy, Joan E. | *A Dictionary of Medical & Related Terms for the Family Historian* (2006) |
| Lincoln, Margarette | *Naval Wives & Mistresses* (2007) |
| May, Trevor | *The Victorian Workhouse* (2005) |
| MacDougall, Philip | *Chatham Past* (1999) |
| Mills, A.D. | *Oxford Dictionary of English Place Names* (1991, 1998) |
| Pappalardo, Bruno | *Tracing your Naval Ancestors* (2003) |
| Pols, Robert | *Dating Nineteenth Century Photographs* (2005) |
| Pope, Dudley | *Life in Nelson's Navy* (1997) |
| Reaney, P.H. | *A Dictionary of English Surnames*, revised third edition by R.M. Wilson (1997) |
| Redmonds, George | *Christian Names in Local and Family History* (2004) |
| Rodger, N.A.M. | *The Wooden World: An Anatomy of the Georgian Navy* (1988) |
| Rodger, N.A.M. | *Naval Records for Genealogists* (1988) |
| Rodger, N.A.M. | *The Command of the Ocean: A Naval History of Britain, 1649-1815* (2004) |
| Titford, John | *Succeeding in Family History: Helpful Hints and Time-saving Tips* (2001) |
| Titford, John | *Writing up Your Family History: A Do-it-yourself Guide* (2003) |

# ADDITIONAL INFORMATION

## ARCHIVES

Number of visits made to each archive or record office in the course of research:

| | |
|---|---|
| Family Records Centre | 67 |
| The National Archives | 52 |
| Society of Genealogists | 44 |
| London Metropolitan Archives | 23 |
| British Library Newspaper Archive | 11 |
| Medway Archives and Local Studies Centre | 7 |
| The History Shop, Wigan | 3 |
| Probate Search Room | 3 |
| Dorset History Centre | 2 |
| Caird Library, National Maritime Museum, Greenwich | 1 |
| Guildhall Library | 1 |
| Chatham Library | 1 |
| The Historic Dockyard, Chatham | 1 |
| Lloyd's Register Group Services Ltd. | 1 |

## ORGANISATIONS

To assist my research, I joined the following organisations:

Cornwall Family History Society
Dorset Family History Society

Kent Family History Society
Manchester & Lancashire Family History Society
North West Kent Family History Society
Society of Genealogists
Somerset & Dorset Family History Society

## CHATHAM

Chatham is a very old town with a history dating back to since records began. The Roman Watling Street passed through the settlement, linking the area to other parts of the country. The settlement itself was first recorded in 880CE as *Cetham,* derived from the British root *Ceto* and the Old English *Ham* meaning 'a homestead or village close to a wood'. In the Domesday Book it is recorded as *Ceteham.*

*High Street Chatham about 1898*

After the Norman Conquest of 1066 the manor of Chatham was given by William the Conqueror to Earl Godwinson.

Chatham appears to have remained a small village until the 16th century, when the sheltered waters of the Medway River became a popular haven for ships. During the reign of Queen Elizabeth I the potential for a naval dockyard and shipbuilding site was recognised, and in 1568 the Royal Naval Dockyard of Chatham was established.

This event was to change the small town out of all recognition. Many skilled shipwrights moved to the area, but there was also a need for large numbers of unskilled labourers. The population rose rapidly over the years as the dockyard expanded its activities and workers poured into the town. In 1831 the population was recorded as more than 16,000.

In 1667 the Dutch carried out a surprise attack on the dockyard and town of Chatham. It was quickly realised that Upnor Fort, built in 1567, was inadequate to defend the dockyard and that a better defence of the area was badly needed. As a result a string of forts was built along the banks of the Medway River, including Fort Amherst. To man the forts, soldiers were moved into the town and barracks were established. All this meant that the basic facilities of the town were stretched to the full. The houses were overcrowded and the sewerage system could not cope at times. All this produced an unhealthy environment and there were frequent outbreaks of disease. Added to this problem were the drinking houses and brothels that sprang up to provide recreation for the soldiers, sailors and workers who roamed the town. Chatham grew to have a bad reputation, and for a time it was considered not such a nice place to live, quite unlike its neighbour Rochester, a short distance away.

In the early 1800s a fire swept through the town, destroying many of the wooden houses.

The situation began to improve in the Victorian period as the authorities in Chatham initiated programmes to eliminate some of the problems. Meanwhile the dockyard continued to increase in size. Scores of ships where built there, including HMS *Victory*, famous for its role in the Battle of Trafalgar.

The railway came to Chatham in 1858 and linked the town with London and the rest of Kent. Trams appeared on the streets quite early, providing local transport. The Victorian architects designed elegant buildings such as the town hall, completed in 1900, and helped to give the town its character.

Many well-known people have been associated with Chatham, including Charles Dickens, who lived there as a boy and liked the town so much that he returned there as an adult.

The years after the Second World War saw many changes in Chatham. The dockyard closed in 1984 and is now a museum depicting the history and activities of the former complex. As in many other towns, an indoor shopping centre was built, taking a great deal of the character away from the former high street. With the formation of Medway Council in 1998 the old town hall became redundant. Thankfully it was saved and is now a theatre and arts centre. Sadly the delightful parish church of St Mary, which stands on the banks of the Medway, is no longer in use. For a while it served as a heritage centre, but now it stands empty and forlorn. Chatham lost its independence in the 1970s with the district changes that took place throughout the UK. It is now part of the Borough of Medway.

## WIGAN

The town of Wigan was once in the county of Lancashire, but with the changes that took place in the 1970s it became part of Greater Manchester. The town stands on the River Douglas and is approximately 8 miles from Bolton, 16 miles from Manchester and 176 miles from London.

The source of the name Wigan is shrouded in the past. Some sources suggest that the name means 'village' or 'settlement'; another theory is that the name is of Celtic origin. It is sometimes thought that the original people to settle in the Wigan area were the Brigantes, a Celtic tribe who occupied a large part of Northern England. Most certainly the Romans occupied the area, because a number of Roman artefacts have been found in the town. Not a great deal is known about Wigan in the Anglo-Saxon period. Scandinavians settled in the area in the 10th century, and it is believed that names like Scholes, derived from the Scandinavian *skali*, meaning 'hut' or 'shed', date from this period of Wigan's history.

Wigan does not appear in the Domesday Book, but historians believe that there is a logical reason for this. It is quite possible that Wigan was included in the barony of Neweton (now Newton-le-Willows). It is thought that the church mentioned in the manor of Neweton could be Wigan parish church. All Saints church itself is very old; parts of the current structure date back to at least the 17th century, though further rebuilding took place in the 1840s.

History tells us that Wigan was probably incorporated as a borough around 1246, as a result of a charter issued by King Henry III. At one time Wigan was one of four boroughs in Lancashire with Royal charters, the others being Lancaster, Liverpool and Preston.

Wigan has its own minor stately home, Haigh Hall, which is surrounded by a 250-acre country park. The present hall was built in the 1840s on the site of a much older structure. There is a well-known legend connected to the hall. Apparently Lady Mabel Bradshaigh or Bradshaw, wife of Sir William Bradshaigh, committed bigamy unintentionally by marrying again, believing her husband to be dead when he failed to come back from the crusades. When Sir William returned after a 10-year campaign, he murdered Lady Mabel's new husband. Though seemingly innocent, as a penance Lady Mabel was condemned to walk barefoot once a week for the rest of her life from her home to a stone cross in the centre of

Wigan. It is not known if the story is true or if she ever underwent the ordeal, but the cross still stands in Wigan and is known as 'Mab's Cross'.

During the English Civil War the town of Wigan was the site of one of the battles of the conflict. The Battle of Wigan Lane took place in 1651 between the Royalists, led by the Earl of Derby, and Cromwell's Parliamentarians, under the command of Colonel Robert Lilburne. The Royalists lost the battle and Wigan fell to Cromwell's army.

Coal was first mined in quantity in Wigan during the 15th century, and the industry quickly grew in size. At its peak Wigan was surrounded by coal mines, making it an important centre for the industry. This prosperity was shared by the textile industry. During the early part of the 19th century the first steam powered cotton mills appeared and quickly multiplied to make Wigan one of the main 'cotton towns' of Lancashire.

This prosperity led to a large increase in the town's population. The industries attracted workers from other parts of the country, and they had to be housed. As a result rows of small houses were rapidly created, often built by the mill owners for their workers. Little planning was involved and the result was a warren of small, uninteresting streets, their houses entered directly from the pavement and separated by narrow cobbled roadways. Often the houses were built back to back with no rear entrance, and with toilets at the end of the street. Prior to its industrialisation Wigan was described as a 'pretty market town'. By 1911 the description had changed to 'an industrial town with its industries filling the atmosphere with smoke'.

For many years, working conditions in both the coal mines and cotton mills were poor. Low pay, long hours, child labour and often a dangerous environment were common in the early days, coupled with the constant shadow of poverty and unemployment at times due to outside forces. It was not until well into the 1800s that conditions began to improve for the workers.

The prosperity of Wigan produced a need for transport, and in the 1790s the town was linked to the Leeds and Liverpool canal system. The railways made an early appearance, and in the 1830s Wigan became one of the first towns in Britain to be served by a railway, linking the town by rail to Manchester, Liverpool and Preston.

The latter part of the Victorian period saw a great many other amenities improved for the citizens of Wigan. A new cemetery was created in 1856, and the infirmary opened its doors in 1873. A new town hall was built in 1867, followed by the market hall in 1877. Mesnes Park was opened to the public in 1878, and in the same year the town had a public library. In 1901 electric trams made an appearance on the streets. The town had already had gas lighting since the 1820s.

A number of well-known people are connected with Wigan, including the entertainer George Formby and the comedian Ted Ray. George Orwell put Wigan in the spotlight with his book *The Road to Wigan Pier*. Michael Marks, the Polish immigrant who arrived in this country unable to speak English and eventually co-founded the Marks and Spencer empire, lived in Wigan for a while. Thomas Beecham of 'Beecham's Pills' fame started his business in Wigan.

Wiganers are occasionally referred to as 'Pie-Eaters'. However, this has nothing to do with eating pies. The term dates back to the 1920s when the miners went on strike for more pay. Some miners were forced to return to work in order to feed their families, and they became known as 'pie-eaters' because they had eaten 'humble pie'.

During the 20th century the prosperity that had made Wigan famous started to decline. From the 1950s on the steady lack of demand for home-produced cotton heralded the closure of the cotton mills. The coal-mining industry suffered the same fate and the collieries that had provided so much employment in the past also closed.

It says much for the resilience of the population that Wigan, far from being defeated by these events, started to reinvent itself and has arisen today as a bright and vibrant town. Service industries have replaced cotton and coal. Tourism has also emerged, and some former cotton mills are now museums to Wigan's past. The once-joked-about Wigan Pier is now a tourist attraction.

In the sporting world, Wigan is frequently in the news with top-rate football and rugby teams.

## OULTON HALL

Oulton Hall was originally owned during the 18th century by a family called Blayds, who were wealthy merchants from Leeds. John Blayds developed the estate but had no children to inherit his property when he died. As a result his will left the estate to his partner John Calverley, on condition that he change his name to John Blayds. Calverley carried out the request and set about remodelling and improving the hall.

A serious fire in 1850 resulted in Oulton Hall having to be rebuilt. Various new features were added at the same time.

During World War I the Calverley family allowed the hall to be used as a hospital and convalescent home for wounded soldiers. In 1925 the family sold the hall and grounds to Yorkshire County Council, and it was used as a mental hospital until 1971.

In 1974 the hall was bought by West Yorkshire Police for use as their headquarters, but this never happened and the hall fell into disrepair.

In spite of ownership returning to the council in 1986, the building was allowed to become almost derelict.

In 1991 De Vere Hotels acquired the lease and as a result Oulton Hall was returned to its past glory and became a five-star hotel. The grounds were laid out again as near as possible to the original.

HANSFORD MISCELLANY

In the course of my research I came across the following, which, though as yet I have not been able to establish a connection to my family, I thought were interesting enough to include:

## Hansford County

Hansford County is located in the US state of Texas. It was named after John M. Hansford, a Texas state congressman and judge. At the last count the population was 5,369.

## The Battle of Trafalgar

It appears from naval records that none of the ships on which James Hansford senior served were called for service at the Battle of Trafalgar. However, a George Hansford did serve on one of the ships that took part in the great naval engagement: HMS *Conqueror*. He received the Naval General Service Medal with Trafalgar clasp in 1847.

The main qualities the family historian needs are

# Dedication

# Patience

# Imagination